The Armada Campaign 1588

1588

The Great Enterprise against England

Campaign • 86

The Armada Campaign 1588

The Great Enterprise against England

Angus Konstam · Illustrated by Howard Gerrard

First published in Great Britain in 2001 by Osprey Publishing,
Midland House, West Way, Botley, Oxford OX2 0PH, UK
44-02 23rd St, Suite 219, Long Island City, NY 11101, USA
Email: info@ospreypublishing.com

Osprey Publishing is part of the Osprey Group.

Transferred to digital print on demand 2010

First published 2001
2nd impression 2008

Printed and bound by Cadmus Communications, USA

A CIP catalogue record for this book is available from the British Library

ISBN: 978 1 84176 192 3

Editorial by Anita Hitchings
Design by The Black Spot
Colour bird's-eye view illustrations by The Black Spot
Cartography by The Map Studio
Battlescene artwork by Howard Gerrard
Originated by Grasmere Digital Imaging Ltd, Leeds, UK

Artist's note

Readers may care to note that the original paintings from which the colour plates in this book were prepared are available for private sale. All reproduction copyright whatsoever is retained by the Publishers. All enquiries should be addressed to:

Howard Gerrard
11 Oaks Road
Tenterden
Kent
TN30 6RD
UK

The Publishers regret that they can enter into no correspondence upon this matter.

The Woodland Trust

Osprey Publishing is supporting the Woodland Trust, the UK's leading woodland conservation charity, by funding the dedication of trees.

www.ospreypublishing.com

Page 2
Spanish soldiers of the late 16th century. This detail from a courtyard mural depicts the troops that would have spearheaded any landing on the English coast. The entire mural celebrated Spanish martial achievements in the Mediterranean and the Azores. (Palacio de el Viso del Marquess, Ciudad Reál)

Page 3
One of the most popular representations of the Armada battle. In the foreground is a Spanish galleass, one of four which include the San Lorenzo and the Girona. *The English and Spanish fleets engaged,* 1588. Oil painting, English school, late 16th century. (NMM – BHC0262)

KEY TO MILITARY SYMBOLS

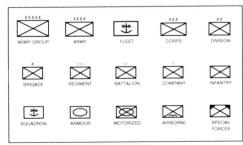

CONTENTS

THEATRE OF OPERATIONS, 1588

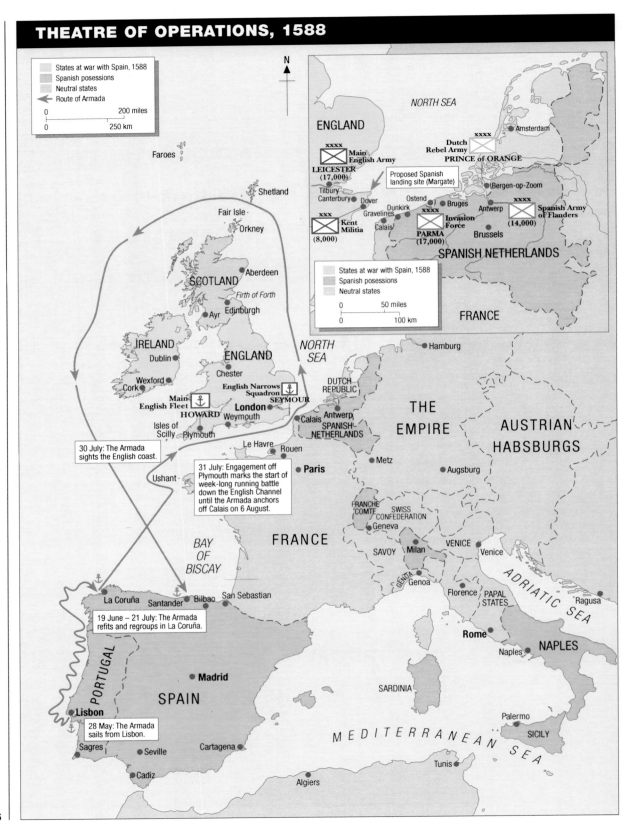

Legend:
- States at war with Spain, 1588
- Spanish posessions
- Neutral states
- → Route of Armada

0 — 200 miles
0 — 250 km

N

North Sea inset map:

ENGLAND

NORTH SEA

Amsterdam

xxxx
Dutch
Rebel Army
PRINCE of ORANGE

xxxx
Main
English Army
LEICESTER
(17,000)

Proposed Spanish
landing site (Margate)

Tilbury
Canterbury
Dover

Ostend
Bruges

Antwerp

xxxx
Spanish Army
of Flanders
(14,000)

Bergen-op-Zoom

xxx
Kent
Militia
(8,000)

Dunkirk
Gravelines
Calais

xxxx
Invasion
Force
PARMA
(17,000)

Brussels

SPANISH NETHERLANDS

FRANCE

States at war with Spain, 1588
Spanish posessions
Neutral states

0 — 50 miles
0 — 100 km

Main map labels:

Faroes

Shetland

Fair Isle
Orkney

SCOTLAND

Aberdeen

Firth of Forth
Edinburgh
Ayr

IRELAND
Dublin
Wexford
Cork

Chester

ENGLAND

NORTH
SEA

English Narrows
Squadron
SEYMOUR

Main
English Fleet
HOWARD
London
Weymouth

Isles of
Scilly
Plymouth

Le Havre
Rouen

Paris

Metz

DUTCH
REPUBLIC

Calais
Antwerp
SPANISH
NETHERLANDS

THE
EMPIRE

AUSTRIAN
HABSBURGS

Hamburg

Augsburg

FRANCHE
COMTE
SWISS
CONFEDERATION
Geneva

FRANCE

SAVOY
Milan
VENICE
Venice

GENOA
Genoa
Florence

PAPAL
STATES

ADRIATIC SEA

Ragusa

Ushant

BAY
OF
BISCAY

La Coruña
Santander
Bilbao
San Sebastian

Rome
Naples

NAPLES

PORTUGAL

Madrid

SPAIN

SARDINIA

Palermo

SICILY

Lisbon

Sagres
Seville
Cartagena

MEDITERRANEAN SEA

Cadiz
Algiers

Tunis

Annotation boxes:

30 July: The Armada
sights the English coast.

31 July: Engagement off
Plymouth marks the start of
week-long running battle
down the English Channel
until the Armada anchors
off Calais on 6 August.

19 June – 21 July: The Armada
refits and regroups in La Coruña.

28 May: The Armada
sails from Lisbon.

INTRODUCTION

LEFT **The Armada's primary mission was to rendezvous with the Duke of Parma's invasion force stationed in the Spanish Netherlands. While a screen of veteran troops watched the Dutch rebels, Parma's troops would cross from Flanders to Kent, protected by the ships of the Armada. As France was neutral (although Catholic), communications between Spain and Flanders were difficult, and relied on a tortuous route through Spanish territories in Italy and the Franche Comte. By contrast, the English were in constant communication with their Protestant Dutch allies. Once the Armada was forced away from the Flemish coast on 8 August, contrary winds forced it to return to Spain around the British Isles. Scotland was neutral (though Protestant), while Catholic Ireland was occupied by English troops. The inset shows the disposition of troops in Flanders, Kent and Holland during early August, 1588.**

osterity records the defeat of the Spanish Armada as the triumph of a small maritime nation who took on a mighty world empire and won a glorious victory. It was seen to mark the beginning of an Elizabethan 'golden age' of exploration, naval glory and overseas colonisation. The Spanish defeat preserved the Protestant Reformation, established England as a leading sea-force and caused the first cracks in the bastion of Spanish world power. Today the pantheon of Elizabethan sea dogs who participated in the campaign have become the creatures of legend. Drake, Hawkins, Frobisher and Raleigh are symbolic of a romanticised view of Elizabethan England, set on patriotic pedestals by centuries of historians.

Any objective study of the campaign reveals that the participants certainly did not realise that they lived in a 'golden age'. Decades of

RIGHT **Philip II of Spain (1527-98). Oil by Alonso Sánchez Collo. This rare portrayal shows the monarch wearing tournament armour. In most paintings he is depicted wearing plain black clothing. Philip was the true architect of the 'Enterprise of England'. (Glasgow Museums and Art Galleries)**

religious persecution and xenophobia in England had done a great deal to influence people and the course of events, while the 'Good Queen Bess' of popular legend was in reality a shrewd political manipulator, assisted by a powerful police and intelligence service. As for the Spanish, Philip II of Spain saw his 'Great Enterprise' as a solution for most of the ills that afflicted Spain. These included a vicious and costly revolt in the Netherlands, the arrival of European interlopers in the New World and a steadily decreasing revenue from the Americas. Philip was at least the political equal of Elizabeth, and the campaign was the climax of two decades of political one-upmanship, in which the stakes were becoming higher and higher. For Elizabeth in 1588, her very survival was at stake.

The Spanish Armada campaign ranks as one of the most fascinating maritime engagements of all time. Two powerful fleets fought a series of battles that transformed naval warfare. In the 16th century no firm tactical doctrines had been established, so the campaign became a test bed for two conflicting theories of war at sea. Although much has been made of the English superiority in gunnery, the English fleet was unable to break the tight defensive formation of the Spanish fleet until a fireship attack scattered the Spanish ships. For their part the Spanish showed great resolution and bravery throughout the fighting. It is also apparent that the Spanish Armada almost succeeded. England was saved less by her 'sea dogs' than by eight tired old merchant ships, poor Spanish communications and a storm, which took everyone by surprise. The historical ramifications of a Spanish victory are almost too huge to comprehend. As historian Geoffrey Parker put it, with no English colonies in America and India, 'the Empire of Philip II on which the sun never set would have remained the largest the world had ever seen'.

ORIGINS OF THE CAMPAIGN

In July 1554 Philip, heir to the Spanish throne, married Mary Tudor, Queen of England. Although the principal aim was to form a political union against France, the marriage also strengthened Mary's position against the Protestants within her own kingdom. Relations between the consort and the Queen's subjects soured rapidly, particularly with the widespread and unpopular persecution of Protestants by 'Bloody Mary'. This was blamed in part on the Spanish, as was an unlucky war with France. Following Mary's death in 1558, Philip and his Spanish advisers were in a precarious situation. The succession remained in question for several months, with the main contenders being Mary's Protestant half-sister Elizabeth, and the Catholic Mary, Queen of Scots. As Mary was a French princess, Philip supported Elizabeth's claim, as the lesser of two evils. When Elizabeth succeeded to the throne in late 1558 (she was crowned in January 1559) she pursued a policy of neutrality and made peace with Spain, while encouraging rivalry between the French and Spanish courts. She also re-introduced Protestantism as the state religion in 1559, and supported the Protestant cause in Scotland.

This period of neutrality came to an end with the start of the Dutch revolt against Spanish rule in 1566. Although a powerful Spanish army crushed the rebellion, tension increased to new levels, precipitated by two further crises. In 1567 a group of Scottish Protestant nobles rebelled against Mary, Queen of Scots and imprisoned her. The following year she escaped to England and threw herself on the mercy of Elizabeth, who

The burning of Protestant martyrs during the reign of Mary I of England. Her death in 1558 marked a shift in policy, and her Protestant sister Elizabeth became a staunch advocate of the Reformation. (Author's collection)

This satirical cartoon depicts Philip II sitting astride a cow (representing the Netherlands). The animal is being fed by Queen Elizabeth, and steadied by the Dutch Prince William of Orange. Spanish and French courtiers are also shown 'interfering' with affairs in the Spanish Netherlands. Engraving, c.1570. (Hensley Collection, Ashville, NC)

promptly imprisoned her. This was seen as an outrage by most Catholics, which Elizabeth only compounded by confiscating five Spanish ships which had been forced to seek refuge in an English port in late 1568. They contained the pay chest for the Spanish Army of Flanders, and Elizabeth kept both the ships and the money. Then in 1568 an English trading expedition to the Americas led by John Hawkins was attacked and mauled at San Juan de Ulúa on the Gulf of Mexico. The survivors included Hawkins and the young Francis Drake, and their return to England in 1569 prompted a national outcry. The stakes had been raised, and when the Pope excommunicated Elizabeth in 1570 he called on all loyal Catholics to oppose her. The following year a Spanish-backed plot against the Queen was uncovered (the Ridolfi conspiracy), and Mary, Queen of Scots was implicated in the intrigue that followed.

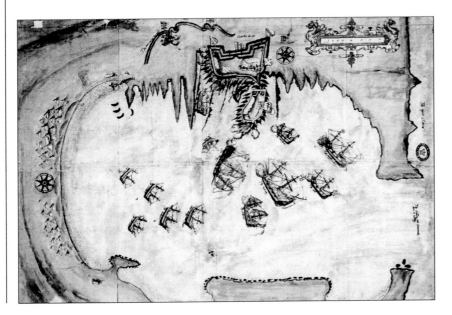

In November 1580 the Spanish launched an ill-conceived and poorly executed attack on Ireland. The small Spanish force was besieged at Smerwick Bay and forced to capitulate. This contemporary map shows naval guns (with four-wheeled truck carriages) being landed from the English ships and dragged into place in the siege lines. (PRO, London – MPF 75)

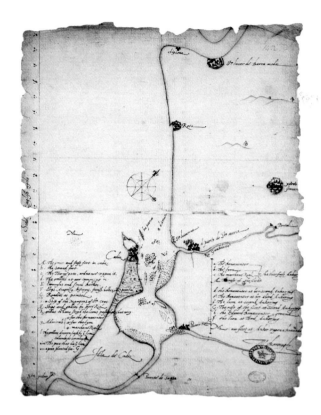

Plan of Drake's attack on Cadiz Harbour, April 1587. Drake's raid was an attempt to disrupt Armada preparations, and his actions were described as having 'singed the King of Spain's beard'. Pen and wash by William Borough, c.1588. (PRO, London – MPF 318)

From 1572 Queen Elizabeth openly encouraged her sea dogs in privateering attacks on Spanish ports and shipping. This culminated in Drake's voyage of circumnavigation (1577-80) when the privateer returned with a fortune in Spanish plunder and was knighted for his efforts. The Spanish were also becoming more aggressive. The year 1572 saw a resurgence of the Dutch rebellion, and in four years the rebel leader William of Orange secured a Protestant enclave in Holland. King Philip responded in 1578 by sending the Duke of Parma to the Spanish Netherlands at the head of a large army. Within two years he had regained control of most of Flanders and was poised for an attack on the key Protestant strongholds in Brabant.

In 1580 Philip also supported an Irish Catholic rising against English rule, and transported 'volunteers' to Smerwick Bay, south-west Ireland, in Spanish ships. While this was under way he launched an attack on Portugal, and by the end of 1580 he had captured both the great port of Lisbon and the Portuguese fleet.

The war continued in the Azores, with the Spanish defeat of a Franco-Portuguese rebel fleet at the Battle of São Miguel in 1582. The Spanish then captured the stronghold of Portuguese resistance at Terceira in the Azores the following year and appeared in the ascendancy, having conquered Portugal while Parma was successfully pushing back the Dutch rebels. In the Treaty of Joinville (1584) the Spanish agreed to support the French Catholics against their Protestant rivals, and the following year the rebel port of Antwerp fell to Parma's troops.

Elizabeth and her advisers felt isolated but could not abandon their Dutch Protestant allies. In August 1585, Elizabeth signed an alliance with the Dutch, promising them military and economic aid. This Treaty of Nonsuch (1585) marked the start of unrestrained hostilities. The 'cold war' of the previous few years had suddenly become a full-scale conflict.

One of the stated aims of Philip was to depose Elizabeth I in favour of Mary, Queen of Scots. Proof of Mary's involvement in the Babington conspiracy of 1586 was enough for Elizabeth, and reluctantly she signed Mary's death warrant. In February 1587, Mary, Queen of Scots was executed, giving Philip II the final justification he needed to attack Elizabethan England.

Although diplomats still sought a way to end the hostilities, preparations were made for an invasion of England, the largest maritime and amphibious operation of the period. The Armada's presence was well known in England, and in April 1587 Drake launched a pre-emptive strike against Cadiz, which the privateer claimed had 'singed the King of Spain's beard'. It cost the Spanish 24 ships, and the Armada was delayed for several months while its commander, the Marquis of Santa Cruz, pursued the sea dog. However, Drake could not prevent the inevitable: as the Duke of Parma readied his army in Flanders and Santa Cruz prepared the invasion fleet in Lisbon, the English could do little other than prepare for the Spanish onslaught.

CHRONOLOGY

1584
June — Marquis de Santa Cruz appointed as Spain's 'Admiral of the Ocean Sea'
December — Treaty of Joinville signed between Spain and France

1585
May — Philip II places an embargo on all trade with England
August — Antwerp captured from the Dutch rebels by the Duke of Parma's army
November — Drake attacks Santiago in the Cape Verde Islands
December — Elizabeth I sends the Earl of Leicester with troops to assist the Dutch rebels

1586
January — Drake sacks Santo Domingo, the capital of Hispaniola (Dominican Republic)
Philip II orders plans for the invasion of England
March — Drake captures Cartagena on the Spanish Main
July — Invasion plan approved and sent to the Duke of Parma
November — Preparations start; ships and supplies are gathered

1587
February — Mary, Queen of Scots is executed on the orders of Elizabeth I of England
April — Drake 'singes the King of Spain's beard' by attacking Cadiz
May — The Armada begins to assemble in Lisbon
June — Drake captures a Spanish treasure galleon off the Azores
July — Philip II and the Pope agree on the government of a Catholic England
September — Santa Cruz arrives in Lisbon to supervise preparations
Final revisions to invasion plan are made

1588
9 February — Marquis of Santa Cruz dies in Lisbon
26 February — Duke of Medina Sidonia accepts command of the Armada
1 April — Final orders sent by Philip II to both Parma and Medina Sidonia
9 May — Armada inspected by Medina Sidonia and deemed ready to sail
28 May — The Spanish Armada sails from Lisbon
3 June — The English fleet gathers in Plymouth
19 June — Bad weather forces Armada to put into La Coruña in north-west Spain
4 July — English fleet sails to launch pre-emptive attack on Spanish fleet
5 July — Dutch fleet blockades Parma's invasion force at Dunkirk
19 July — The English fleet return to Plymouth due to bad weather
21 July — Spanish Armada sets sail from La Coruña
25 July — Galley squadron forced to put into French port
29 July — The Armada is sighted by an English scouting vessel
30 July — The Spanish Armada sights the Lizard on the Cornish coast
Medina Sidonia holds a council of war
The English fleet puts to sea from Plymouth
31 July — Battle off Plymouth
Both the *San Salvador* and the *Nuestra Señora de Rosario* are damaged
Drake abandons the fleet to pursue the damaged Spanish vessel *Rosario*

1 August	The Armada re-forms off Start Point
	English ships capture the *San Salvador*
2 August	Battle off Portland
3 August	The English reorganise their fleet into four divisions
	The Spanish Armada approaches the Isle of Wight
4 August	Battle off the Isle of Wight
	The Armada is now committed to anchorage off Calais
6 August	Armada anchors off Calais
7 August	Fireship attack planned
	Medina Sidonia learns that Parma's invasion force is not ready
8 August	Fireship attack scatters the Spanish Armada
	Galleass *San Lorenzo* captured off Calais
	Battle of Gravelines
9 August	Armada forced to abandon rendezvous with Parma
	Council of war held on Spanish flagship elects to sail home around Scotland
10 August	Army of Flanders ready to embark, but the invasion is cancelled
	Main English fleets pursues the Spanish Armada northwards
	Seymour's squadron returns to the Downs
13 August	Armada now level with the Firth of Forth in Scotland
	English fleet abandons the pursuit of the Armada
18 August	Elizabeth I addresses her troops at Tilbury
20 August	Armada passes Orkney and Shetland and enters the Atlantic
21 August	Medina Sidonia sends messenger to Philip II with news of his failure
31 August	Parma abandons his invasion attempts and resumes war against Dutch
14 September	Storms lash the Irish coast; start of two weeks of bad weather
21 September	Height of the 'Armada Storm'; numerous shipwrecks on Irish coast
	Medina Sidonia arrives in Santander
24 September	Philip II told of the failure of his 'Grand Enterprise'
30 September	Worst of the storm passes to the north of Ireland
	Shipwreck survivors scattered throughout Ireland are rounded up by English
28 October	De Leiva drowned during shipwreck of the galleass *Girona* off Ireland
10 November	Full extent of tragedy revealed to Philip II, who prays for death
12 November	Spanish decide to continue the war against England
24 November	Queen Elizabeth attends a service of thanksgiving in London

THE OPPOSING COMMANDERS

THE SPANISH

Don Alvaro de Bazán, 1st Marquis of Santa Cruz (1526-88), was the original architect of the Spanish Armada. He was already an experienced naval commander, having fought at Lepanto (1571) and the Azores (1582). A skilled administrator, he drew together the forces needed for the enterprise, although he remained opposed to the King's scaling down of the expedition, which incorporated a rendezvous with the Spanish Army in Flanders rather than shipping the troops from Lisbon. At 62, the marquis was old for such an important command, but his drive was apparent in the efforts he made to ready the fleet, fighting corruption, malaise and royal interference in equal measure. If he had actually led the Armada into battle, it is unlikely that he would have failed to deliver the fleet intact to the Flemish rendezvous, and he might even have been able to keep it there while the army embarked. When the marquis died, in Lisbon in February 1588, the ultimate success of the Armada was placed in jeopardy.

Don Alonso Pérez de Guzmán el Bueno, 7th Duke of Medina Sidonia (1550-1619), was appointed as the new commander of the Armada within days of the death of the Marquis of Santa Cruz. The head of one of the richest and most powerful aristocratic houses in Spain, he has been described as honest, pious and magnanimous. He was also a highly intelligent man, although relatively inexperienced in naval warfare. When he was appointed, he wrote to the king pleading ill health and lack of financial resources, and although he eventually accepted the command, this reluctance has cast a doubt over his suitability for the task. He displayed great personal courage during the campaign, and kept the Armada intact as it sailed up the English Channel, but he was not really up to the challenges the command thrust upon him. His flagship was the *San Martín* (1,000 tons).

Juan Martinez de Recalde (1526-88) was born in Bilbao, northern Spain. He served as a royal official for 20 years, overseeing shipping between Bilbao and the Spanish Netherlands. During this period he gained extensive maritime experience commanding royal vessels, and in 1572 King Philip II placed him in command of the fleet bound for Flanders. He remained in Flanders for the next eight years to command Spanish naval forces and fight Dutch 'sea beggars'. In 1580 Recalde escorted the Spanish amphibious expedition to Smerwick in Ireland, and in 1582–83 he commanded a squadron in the Azores campaign. By 1588 he was seen as one of Spain's most experienced naval commanders. During the campaign he consistently proved himself as the best tactical commander

TOP **Don Alvaro de Bazán, 1st Marquis of Santa Cruz (1526-88). This Spanish nobleman was the original commander of the Armada, but he died before the fleet sailed from Lisbon. Despite his age, he was an aggressive and competent leader. (Author's collection)**

ABOVE **Don Alonso Pérez de Guzmán, 7th Duke of Medina Sidonia (1550-1619). Although he lacked naval experience, the Spanish Armada commander displayed great tactical skill, making the most of the unsuitable collection of vessels under his command. (Fundación Archivo Casa de Medina Sidonia)**

in the Armada, and was usually found in the thick of the fighting. Although he survived the campaign, he died two weeks after his return to Bilbao, a sick and broken man. If he had commanded the fleet during the campaign, the outcome may well have been different. His flagship was the *San Juan de Portugal* (1,050 tons).

Don Alonso Martínez de Leiva (c.1540-88) was a favourite of the King of Spain, and regarded as the epitome of the Spanish chivalric ideal. Don Alonso had extensive military experience as a soldier, having campaigned in Italy and North Africa. In 1576 he campaigned with Don John of Austria against the Dutch rebels, then returned to Italy and was appointed Captain-General of the Sicilian galleys. As a naval commander he took part in the conquest of Portugal (1580), before being given command of the Milanese cavalry. In 1587 he was given command of the amphibious troops embarked in the Armada. Although he held no formal naval command, Medina Sidonia put Don Alonso in charge of the vanguard squadrons. He also carried a secret document which named him as successor if the Duke were to die (therefore bypassing Recalde). Don Alonso drowned in the galleass *Girona* when it was wrecked off Antrim in October 1588. During the campaign his flagship was *La Rata Santa María Encoronada* (820 tons).

Alessandro Farnese, Duke of Parma (1545-92), was a grandson of King Charles V of Spain, making him a nephew of Philip II. Although born in Parma in Italy, he had been educated in the Spanish court. In 1571 he took part in the Lepanto campaign as an aide-de-camp, and in 1578 he was appointed Governor of the Netherlands. This placed the 38-year-old general in charge of Spain's veteran Army of Flanders, and he displayed considerable martial abilities against the Dutch rebels, recapturing most of Flanders, including the key city of Antwerp. By 1588, when orders came to form part of the 'Great Enterprise' against England, he was engaged in the piece-by-piece conquest of Holland. A skilled soldier and diplomat, he possessed the ability to outwit his English adversaries if he were able to land. Given the elite troops at his disposal, victory would have been almost certain.

THE ENGLISH

Charles Howard, Lord Effingham (1536-1624), was appointed Lord High Admiral in 1585 and in December 1587 he took command of the naval force gathered to counter the Armada. His command style was by necessity based on collaboration, achieved through a regular council of war. He showed little ability to maintain close tactical control over his fleet once it was in action, but instead led by example. Following the campaign he was awarded the earldom of Nottingham. His flagship was the *Ark Royal* (540 tons).

Lord Henry Seymour (1540-c.1600) was appointed as the Admiral of the Narrow Seas Squadron in 1588, becoming Howard's second-in-command. He was an experienced naval leader, having commanded royal squadrons in home waters since the early 1570s. His principal duty

TOP **Juan Martinez de Recalde (1526-88), oil painting by an unknown artist. The most experienced of all the Spanish commanders, the second-in-command favoured a more aggressive strategy than Medina Sidonia, and during the campaign he remained in the thickest of the fighting. (Disputación Floral de Vizcaya, Bilbao)**

ABOVE **Alessandro Farnese, Duke of Parma (1545-92). The Spanish general given the task of providing an invasion force from his veteran Army of Flanders. Poor communications between Parma and Medina Sidonia were the major reason for the failure of the Armada. Oil painting by Otto van Veen. (Musée Royaux de Beaux-Arts de Belgique, Brussels – 1327)**

ABOVE, LEFT **Charles Howard, 2nd Baron Howard of Effingham (1536-1624), from a miniature attributed to Nicholas Hilliard, c.1605. Howard proved an effective commander, but he was unable to break the Spanish formation until after his fireship attack off Calais, on 8 August. (NMM, London)**

ABOVE, CENTRE **Lord Henry Seymour, Admiral of the Narrow Seas, c.1588. Oil painting attributed to the circle of Frederico Zucherro. Seymour's reserve fleet had a double mission: to block any landing attempt by the Duke of Parma and to reinforce Lord Howard when called upon. (Parham Park, West Sussex – 206)**

ABOVE, RIGHT **Sir Francis Drake (c.1540-96). Oil painting by an unknown artist, c.1585. Despite his status as a national hero, Drake was a pirate (or at best a privateer) rather than a naval commander. His pursuit of the lucrative and damaged galleon Rosario off Plymouth threatened to jeopardise Howard's strategy. (National Portrait Gallery, London – 4032)**

was to prevent any landing on the south-east coast by the Duke of Parma's army. His relationship with his cousin Charles Howard was strained, and after the campaign he complained that Howard tried to deprive him of the honour due to him. His participation was restricted to the Battle off the Flemish Banks, but he proved himself a skilled commander. His flagship was the *Rainbow* (384 tons).

Sir Francis Drake (c.1540-96) is the best remembered of all the English naval commanders, known mainly for his career as a privateer. Drake participated in the débâcle at San Juan de Ulúa (1569), then spent the next three years raiding the 'Spanish Main', returning to England a wealthy man. His circumnavigation of the globe earned him even greater wealth (plundered from the Spanish), and he was knighted by a grateful Queen Elizabeth, who called him 'my pirate'. This open support for a man who had illegally attacked the Spanish made war inevitable. Further privateering in the Caribbean (1585/6) was curtailed when Drake was appointed to lead an attack on Cadiz (1587). At the start of the campaign Drake's stock was high and he was regarded as an unofficial second-in-command. His true privateering tendencies were revealed when he chased after the *Rosario* off the Devon coast, in direct contradiction to his orders from Howard. Although he performed well, he was criticised for his lack of discipline. His flagship was the *Revenge* (441 tons).

John Hawkins (1532-95) was a Plymouth merchant who was one of the first interlopers in the Spanish Main. In 1568 his trading squadron was forced to shelter in the Mexican anchorage of San Juan de Ulúa. Before he could leave, the annual Spanish treasure fleet arrived and the Spanish launched a surprise attack. Hawkins barely managed to escape, leaving behind most of his ships and men. In 1578 he was made Treasurer of the Navy and he performed miracles, refitting and modernising the fleet, improving its efficiency and ultimately laying the groundwork for the English victory in the Armada campaign. He was also accused of financial irregularities. During the campaign he helped prepare the fleet for action, then assumed command of a squadron. Although he failed to

distinguish himself, he proved a capable, brave and energetic commander. His flagship was the *Victory* (565 tons).

Martin Frobisher (c.1537-94) was another of the sea dogs whose expertise lay in exploration rather than in privateering. Born in Yorkshire, he had been brought up in London, and participated in slaving expeditions to West Africa. During the 1560s he operated as a privateer before becoming involved in exploration. During the period 1574-77 he undertook three voyages in search of the Northwest Passage, and in 1585/6 he accompanied Drake on his Caribbean adventures. In 1588 he was appointed as one of Howard's squadron commanders, and although he was criticised for his performance off Portland, he showed great spirit. He was knighted by the Lord Admiral during the campaign, but his animosity towards Drake led to a subsequent war of words between the two commanders. His flagship was the *Triumph* (760 tons).

Robert Dudley, Earl of Leicester (c.1532-88), was one of Queen Elizabeth's favourites and a leading courtier, but he lacked any military experience. Nevertheless, he was appointed Governor-General of the English army in the Netherlands in 1586. He returned to England in 1588, and the Queen immediately gave him the command of the army gathered at Tilbury. He died just after the Armada campaign, and Elizabeth was reportedly distraught for weeks after hearing the news. A mediocre commander, he would have been hard-pressed to offer much of a challenge to the Duke of Parma.

ABOVE, LEFT **Sir John Hawkins (1532-95). Oil painting, English School, 1581.** Another of the 'sea dogs' or 'official privateers', Hawkins made a significant contribution to the English victory by his work as a naval administrator in the years preceding the Armada campaign. (NMM – BHC2755)

ABOVE, CENTRE **Sir Martin Frobisher (c.1537-94). Oil painting, 1577, by Cornelius Ketel.** An explorer more than a privateer, Frobisher played a prominent role in the Armada campaign and was knighted for his efforts after the Spanish defeat. (Bodleian Library, Oxford)

ABOVE, RIGHT **Robert Dudley, Earl of Leicester (c.1532-88). Oil painting, English School, c.1586.** As commander of the English army gathered at Tilbury, Dudley had the task of doing battle with the Duke of Parma if the Spanish managed to land in Kent. (Parham Park, West Sussex)

BOTTOM **George Clifford, 3rd Earl of Cumberland (1558-1605). Oil, c.1590, by Nicholas Hilliard.** Clifford was an unsuccessful privateer but proved an able squadron commander during the campaign. After the Battle off Gravelines, he was given the honour of taking the news of the victory to the Queen at Tilbury. (NMM, London - 10.1605)

17

THE OPPOSING FLEETS

THE SPANISH ARMADA

The fleet gathered in Lisbon for Philip II's 'Great Enterprise' consisted of ships from all corners of Spain's European territories and those of her allies. It even included neutral ships which were impounded and commandeered, such as the Scottish vessel *St. Andrew*, which became the *San Andres*. Space precludes a detailed description of the ship types involved, but extensive information is provided in Elite 70: *Elizabethan Sea Dogs 1560-1605*, by the same author, which also includes a summary of contemporary naval tactics and gunnery.

The Armada was divided into squadrons with territorial designations (Portugal, Biscay, etc.) that served as administrative rather than tactical units. Although the original intention was to operate these squadrons as distinct units, after the first battle of Plymouth (31 July), the scheme was abandoned and individual ships were grouped by size and firepower

A Spanish launch recovering an anchor. Detail from a Spanish tapestry depicting the Spanish assault on Tunis (1535). In the middle foreground is a *patache*, one of the small craft used by the Spanish as communication vessels. (Reales Alcazáres, Seville)

rather than by administrative sub-division. In the past, historians have placed too great an emphasis on these units and consequently have encountered problems with the command exercised by the fleet commanders. For example, Martín de Bertendona, who commanded the Levant Squadron, was given command of a 'van', during the battle off Portland (2 August), which consisted of the most powerful ships from several squadrons; Juan Martinez de Recalde was the commander of the Biscay Squadron but sailed in the vice-flag of the Portugal Squadron as deputy fleet commander.

The squadron structure also tended to group similar vessels together. The Portugal Squadron consisted of powerful and well-armed ocean-going galleons captured from the Portuguese in 1580. These ships became the core of the Armada and participated in the forefront of most of the battles in the Channel. The Castille Squadron was composed of galleons earmarked for the annual Treasure Fleets *(Flotas),* which sailed between Seville and the New World. They were robust and low-hulled, designed for transatlantic sailing, where performance was more important than armament. The Levant Squadron was made up of large Mediterranean grain vessels, converted into warships for the campaign. The squadrons of Biscay and Guipúzcoa relied on Spanish merchant vessels from the northern Atlantic seaboard, and these Basque-built ships were regarded as excellent. The Andalusia Squadron used similar vessels from Spain's southern coast. They were less robust ships, but made up for their deficiency by being particularly well armed. The four galleasses came from Naples, and represented a hybrid form of vessel; combining the oar-powered mobility of a galley with the firepower and sails of a galleon. They were clumsy vessels, but proved useful in the light breezes and calms encountered during the Armada's progress down the Channel. The Squadron of Hulks was comprised of bulk merchant ships pressed into service from all over Europe. Ideal for carrying grain, they were not well suited to conversion as warships and so were used to transport stores, troops and supplies for the rest of the fleet. Apart from the four galleys which returned to Spain before the start of the campaign, the rest of the fleet was made up of small vessels used as dispatch boats, scouting vessels and for communication between the ships of the fleet. A popular misconception is that the Armada consisted of large, well-armed galleons. The reality is that it was made up of a hastily gathered force of shipping from all over Europe and that the handful of real warships were augmented by converted merchant vessels. Although it represented the largest concentration of 16th-century shipping ever assembled, it was far from being a homogenous force.

The Spanish relied almost exclusively on a doctrine based on close combat. Although their ships were well armed, they preferred to fire on the enemy in a single devastating volley at point-blank range, then overwhelm their opponent with boarding parties. This was reflected in the composition of the crew, where the seamen were supported by two or three times their number of soldiers. For example, the fleet flagship *San Martín* (a 1,000-ton galleon) carried 161 sailors and 308 soldiers; the *Santiago* (a 520-ton galleon in the same squadron) was crewed by 307 soldiers and only 80 sailors. Spanish naval experience had for the most part been gained through fighting the French, Portuguese and Ottoman Turks, who all relied on similar boarding tactics. If any English

Wooden shot gauges recovered from the wreck of *La Trinidad Valencera*, showing the range of different-sized guns carried on the Spanish ships. Roundshot would be passed through the hoops to ensure the shot would fit into the appropriate gun-barrel. (Ulster Museum, Belfast)

Pen and pencil drawing of a Spanish gun mounted on a 'sea-carriage'. Unlike the four-wheeled truck carriages used by the English, the Spanish retained these less efficient carriages. (Archivo General de Simancas, Valladolid – MPD XVIII-48)

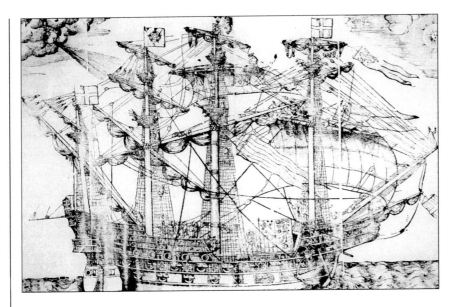

ship was grappled by a large Spanish warship, then this predominance in trained and experienced soldiers would have guaranteed victory. The problem was that throughout the campaign the English refused to let themselves be boarded.

THE ENGLISH FLEET

Like their Spanish opponents, the English fleet consisted of only a small portion of royal warships. Queen Elizabeth I maintained 21 warships of 200 tons or more, and of these, only four had been built in the decade preceding the Armada. These four – the *Revenge,* the *Vanguard,* the *Rainbow* and the fleet flagship *Ark Royal* – were designed from the keel up as 'race-built' galleons, under the supervision of John Hawkins. Compared to Spanish galleons, the English ships had far less super-structure and carried a more homogenous and powerful armament. They were also faster than Spanish vessels of a similar size, and the sail plan of one of them (presumably the *Revenge)* shows a graceful ship which combined power with speed.

The genius of Hawkins as a naval administrator lay in the work he conducted on the rest of the royal fleet. Most of the remaining vessels were carracks; the equivalent of the Spanish *nao,* although designed as warships rather than as merchantmen. The bulk were built during the 1560s, when English naval doctrine was similar to the Spanish, placing an emphasis on the ship as a bastion – a platform from which to fight a boarding action or to repel one. Hawkins instituted an extensive programme of refurbishment and refitting from 1578, and by the time of the Armada campaign they had been transformed into vessels more akin to the latest race-built galleons. Even though they were old and broader in the beam than the latest vessels, they were still faster and more weatherly than any Spanish opponent.

In 1587 the royal shipwrights Peter Pett and Matthew Baker surveyed the entire royal fleet of 34 vessels and proclaimed that several of the

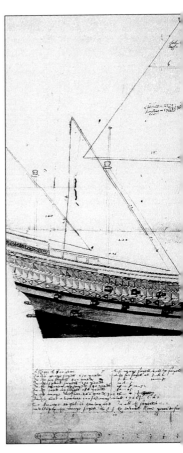

ABOVE LEFT **The *Ark Royal* from a contemporary woodcut. This was the English flagship, commanded by the Lord Admiral, Charles Howard. She was at the forefront of most of the major engagements of the campaign. (British Museum, London – 1874-8-8-1367)**

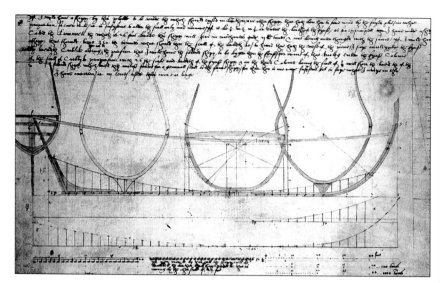

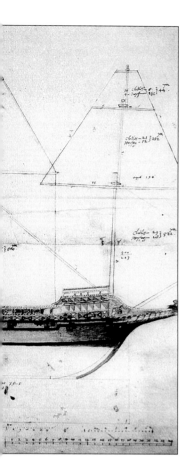

ABOVE **An English 'race-built' galleon, probably drawn by the master-shipwright Matthew Baker, c.1586. Note the bronze guns mounted on four-wheeled truck carriages in the waist of the ship. (Magdalene College, Cambridge)**

ABOVE, RIGHT **Hull cross-sections demonstrating the clean, narrow lines of the new breed of English royal warships. From Matthew Baker's *Fragments of Ancient English Shipwrightry*, 1586. (Magdalene College, Cambridge)**

BELOW, RIGHT **The English warship *White Bear*. Engraving by Claes Jansz. Visscher. This old 1,000-ton carrack was altered as part of Hawkins' modernisation programme, and during the campaign she was commanded by Lord Sheffield. (NMM 8.33)**

older royal warships, such as the *Mary Rose*, built in 1557, were in 'dangerous' condition. She still took an active part in the campaign. Although these royal ships only comprised 18 per cent of the total fleet, they were the best warships afloat, and more than a match for the powerful galleons of the Spanish fleet.

The bulk of the English fleet consisted of merchant vessels bought into the Queen's service for the duration of the campaign. Records concerning the hiring and equipping of these ships are fragmentary, but enough survive to provide an outline of this auxiliary force. One part was a 'volunteer reserve' of armed merchant ships which had volunteered to form part of the fleet; others were simply pressed into service, along with their crews.

Some 30 or so of these armed merchant ships displaced over 200 tons, and carried up to 40 guns, making them the equivalent of

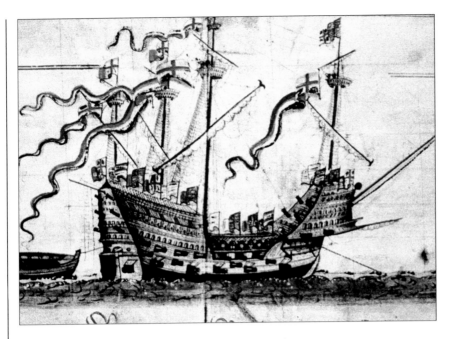

many of the armed merchant vessels in the Spanish fleet. Some were veterans of Drake's privateering expedition to the Spanish Main three years earlier, and others had taken part in the raid on Cadiz in 1587. Many were owned by the senior English commanders or by families connected to them by marital or mercantile bonds. Howard owned seven privateers or armed merchant vessels which took part in the campaign, while Hawkins owned two and Drake three. One problem was that of the 163 private ships which took part in the campaign, 108 displaced less than 100 tons. In the words of Sir William Winter: 'If you had seen what I have seen of the simple service that hath been done by the merchant and coast ships, you would have said that we had been little helped by them, otherwise than that they did make a show.' They were of little practical use in the campaign, but the English were facing an unprecedented threat and any vessel was better than none at all.

The major advantage the English had over the Spaniards was in gunnery. The Spanish relied on an older design of two-wheeled gun carriage for their armament and usually lashed these guns and carriages to the sides of their ships to absorb the recoil when they were fired. By contrast, the English had developed a four-wheeled truck carriage and secured their guns using a system of ropes and pulleys. This type of carriage was first seen on the *Mary Rose* (1545), and continued in use with relatively little variation until well into the 19th century. It allowed the guns to be traversed easily, reloaded more rapidly and operated more efficiently than the guns mounted on Spanish carriages.

This simple advantage, combined with a dearth of 'sea soldiers', dictated English tactics: to avoid boarding and to bombard the Armada using artillery. It was only in the closing battle of the campaign that the English commanders used this to best effect, moving within close range so that every shot would count. The English could effectively outmanoeuvre and outshoot their Spanish opponents, dictating when, where and how the engagement was fought.

THE OPPOSING PLANS

THE SPANISH GRAND DESIGN

I n 1584 the Marquis de Santa Cruz was appointed Captain-General of the Ocean Sea, charged with all operations in the Atlantic Ocean. Even before his appointment he had drawn up suggestions for invasion plans. Following Elizabeth's alliance with the Dutch in 1585, King Philip II wrote to Santa Cruz and the Duke of Parma, asking for detailed plans for an invasion. In the Spring of 1586 they both submitted their proposals, which offered remarkably different solutions to the problem.

The Marquis de Santa Cruz favoured an amphibious operation on a hitherto unimagined scale. A naval force of around 150 major ships would be gathered in Lisbon and transport an army of 55,000 men direct from the Iberian peninsula to England. It would include all artillery, engineering and logistical support the army needed. Once it sailed, the Armada would retain a tight defensive formation, preventing the English from disrupting the fleet's progress to its destination. On reaching the landing site, 200 specially constructed boats would ferry the army ashore, supported by an inshore squadron of 40 galleys and six galleasses which would accompany the Armada. Once the army was ashore it would advance rapidly to crush the English. He never specified a landing site, probably for reasons of secrecy.

The Duke of Parma realised that it would be impossible to keep the plans a secret, so he advocated an unsupported lightning dash across the Channel. A force of 30,000 foot and 500 horse would be transported in invasion barges, landing at a point between Dover and Margate. He

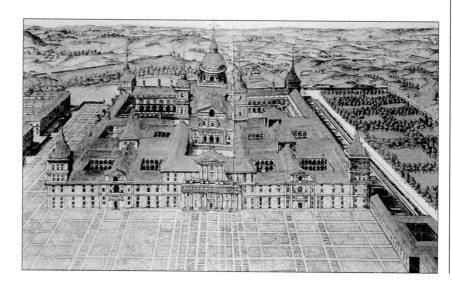

The Escorial Palace outside Madrid served as the headquarters of Philip II of Spain during the planning and execution of the Spanish Armada campaign. Philip ran his empire from a small suite of rooms in the palace but maintained a network of contacts and messengers who kept him in touch with European affairs. (Biblioteca Marucelianna, Florence)

Lisbon served as the embarkation port for the Spanish Armada. During the spring and summer of 1588 this harbour was filled with ships, the docks teeming with men, munitions and supplies. This was the greatest logistical operation ever undertaken during the 16th century. Hand-coloured engraving by Theodore de Bry, c.1570. (Rare Book Division, New York Public Library)

ORDERS,
Set dovvne by the
Duke of Medina, Lord general
of the Kings Fleet, to be obſerued in
the voyage toward England.

Tranſlated out of Spaniſh into Engliſh by T.P.

Imprinted at London by Thomas Orwin for Thomas Gilbert, dwelling in Fleetſtreete neere to the ſigne of the Caſtle. 1588.

ABOVE **An enterprise as huge as the Spanish Armada was impossible to keep secret. This English translation of the Armada's composition, rules of engagement and operational plans was published in London in 1588, before the Spanish fleet had left Lisbon. (Huntingdon Library, San Marino, CA)**

RIGHT **A gun foundry in the Spanish Netherlands. While the Armada was armed with ordnance from all over Europe, the Flemish gun foundries were regarded as some of the best in Europe. Archaeological evidence showed that many Italian, Portuguese and Spanish pieces were of a much poorer quality. (Author's collection)**

estimated the crossing would take between eight and twelve hours. If the English were taken by surprise, he felt the invasion would stand a very great chance of success. If the English fleet blocked the way, Parma expected that a naval force sailing from Lisbon could divert the English from the invasion route to allow a crossing. Once ashore, he had no doubt that his troops could drive on London and brush aside any English opposition.

Philip II reviewed the two plans with his military adviser, Don Juan de Zúñiga, and on 2 April 1586 he ordered the Marquis to gather together

the ships and supplies he needed. Zúñiga then proposed launching both invasions at the same time. The Armada would land a force of around 30,000 men in Ireland, and while the English were diverted, Parma should make his dash across the Channel. Reinforcements would then be brought up from Spain to support the beachheads. Parma vigorously opposed this plan, claiming that the cross-Channel resources should not be wasted on the Irish venture.

Drake's attack on Cadiz in May 1587 forced Philip to alter the plan. Ireland was abandoned, and as less troops were available in Spain, the Armada would have to rendezvous with Parma, then escort his invasion barges. Their orders were to 'sail in the name of God straight to the English Channel and go along it until you have anchored off Margate Head, having first warned the Duke of Parma of your approach'. In effect, the Armada and its troops would support Parma by keeping the crossing areas clear of enemy ships. The Armada was reduced to 130 ships, 30 of which would be small craft displacing under 100 tons. They would transport a force of 17,000 soldiers, and would unite with Parma's invasion force of 17,000 soldiers and 120 barges.

This was a compromise, and the King's plan left many questions unanswered; such as how the Armada would co-ordinate movements with Parma. It also presumed that the Spanish fleet could keep its position in the waters between Dunkirk and Calais for the time it took Parma's men to cross. Furthermore, it failed to suggest what the Armada would do next, apart from anchor in the Thames and wait for the army to crush the English on land.

THE ENGLISH DEFENSIVE STRATEGY

The defence of England was based on her navy. As Sir Walter Raleigh wrote after the campaign: 'An army to be transported by sea … and the [landing] place left to the choice of the invader … cannot be resisted on the coast of England without a fleet to impeach it.'

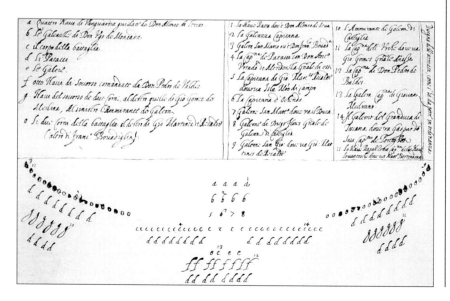

The Armada battle formation was outlined in a letter written to the Duke of Tuscany by his ambassador in Lisbon in May 1588. The detailed plan was amazingly accurate, and reflects the Armada's dispositions as it engaged the English fleet off Plymouth on 31 July. (Archivo di Stato, Florence)

English seamen of the Armada period, shown on the cover of a 'waggoner' (a form of coastal pilot). The frontspiece of The Mariners Mirrour (1588) by Lucas Jansz Waghenaer. Engraving by Theodor de Bry. (NMM, London – D8264)

BELOW **Map of the Dorset coast near Weymouth and Portland Bill, showing the coastal warning beacons, designed to spread the news of any attempted Spanish landing. Detail of a hand-coloured engraving, c.1588. (British Library, London, Department of Manuscripts – Cotton Aug. 1.1.33)**

This neatly summed up Elizabeth's problem: too few experienced troops and too many places to defend.

During the month preceding the invasion, Drake persuaded Howard to move the bulk of the English fleet from the Downs to Plymouth, leaving behind a screening force under Seymour to prevent any attempted 'sneak' invasion by the Duke of Parma. Because of the prevailing westerly winds, a fleet gathered as far west as possible could follow the Armada from windward and harass it all the way down the Channel, rather than simply contesting the Dover Straits (between Dover and Calais). By 3 June the fleet had gathered in Plymouth and the force of 105 ships included 19 royal warships and 46 large, armed merchantmen.

Drake also advocated a pre-emptive strike against La Coruña in Spain, and consequently 60 ships sortied from Plymouth on 4 July. However, bad weather and contrary winds forced Howard and Drake to abandon the enterprise, and the fleet returned to Plymouth. They were still in port on 29 July when news came that the Spanish Armada lay off the Cornish coast.

England's land defences were hastily improvised. A third of all the militia of the southern counties were brought to London, where they formed an army of approximately 21,000 troops, charged with safeguarding the Queen. On 6 July a reserve army was formed at Tilbury in Essex. Commanded by the Earl of Leicester, this force of 17,000 men consisted of militia stiffened by about 4,000 regular troops recently brought back from Holland. A further 29,500 militia guarded the Channel coast from Cornwall to Kent. Of these, just under 9,000 were stationed in Kent itself.

In theory, as the Armada advanced east up the Channel, these county militias were meant to follow it along the coast, so that wherever the Spanish landed, the local militia would be reinforced. A system of warning beacons was set up to convey news of the Armada's progress. In reality, when the Armada passed by, most county militiamen simply

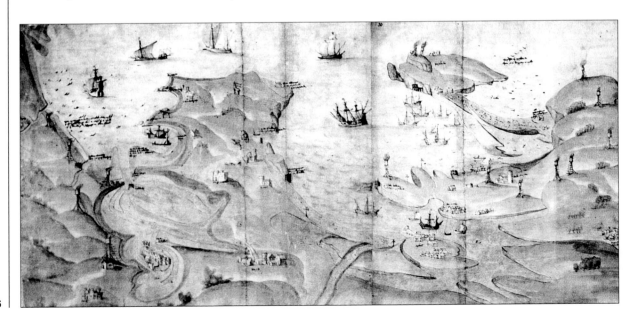

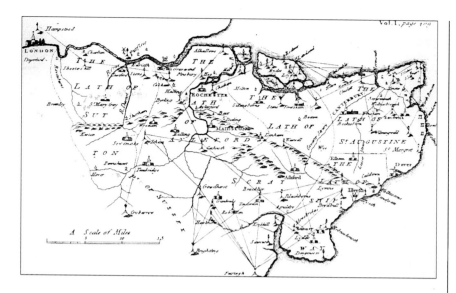

English beacon system, reproduced from *Beacons in Kent*, a manuscript by William Lamarde, c.1585. This was the region earmarked for the landing by the Duke of Parma's veteran army. Apart from the army encamped at Tilbury, the south-east was defended by poorly trained militia and volunteers and a handful of royal coastal forts. (British Library – Add. MS 62935)

returned home. A further 8,000 militia were available from the northern counties, and a similar number from Wales and the Midlands. In the event of a Spanish landing, they were to march and join the main army at London or Tilbury. However, it soon became apparent that the militia were reluctant to fight, particularly in Kent, and thousands deserted during the campaign.

Most militia had little or no training, and inadequate weapons. For example, 10,000 raised in London were issued with bows, although no archery practice had been enforced for almost a century. Above all, they had had no military involvement, and even the regulars were seen as inexperienced. By contrast, the Spanish soldiers of the Army of Flanders were hard-bitten veterans, and the Spanish soldiers carried in the Armada had military experience. As the historian Geoffrey Parker surmised, with inadequate coastal defences, a poorly trained and ill-equipped army and ineffective generals, the English would have been hard pressed to put up much opposition to the Spanish if they had managed to land. Parker estimated that Parma could have captured Kent and London in two weeks, and even without further campaigning could have forced Elizabeth to sign a humiliating peace treaty.

THE CAMPAIGN

THE LAUNCH OF THE 'GREAT ENTERPRISE'

On 9 February 1588 the Marquis de Santa Cruz died in Lisbon, the victim of overwork and chronic illness. The King appointed the Duke of Medina Sidonia as his replacement, and after initial reservations the Duke accepted the post. Preparations for the Armada were in turmoil, and only a handful of the men, ships and stores were ready. Under supervision, Lisbon was transformed as new ships arrived; others were repaired and provisioned, and the Portuguese gun foundries worked at full production. By May each of the 130 ships of the expedition was issued with an adequate provision of ordnance, powder and shot, stores were loaded, pilots issued with the appropriate charts and each ship was inspected, and refitted where appropriate. A total of 18,973 soldiers were embarked, together with their military equipment, including a full siege train. The Duke infused the fleet with a new sense of optimism, and on 9 May the fleet was inspected and declared ready for sea. Bad weather kept it in Lisbon harbour for another fortnight, but on 28 May the Spanish Armada slipped anchor and headed out into the Atlantic. Philip II's 'Great Enterprise' had begun.

From the first the Armada's progress was dogged by weather 'boisterous and bad as if it were December' and the squadron of hulks

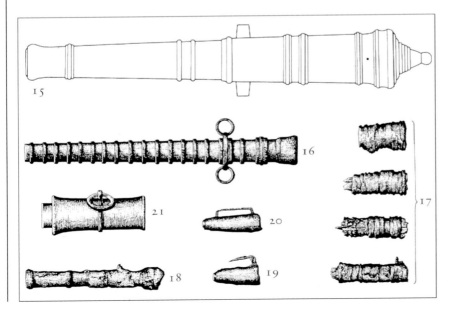

A selection of iron guns recovered from Spanish Armada wrecks. The top drawing is of a cast-iron *sacre* recovered from *El Gran Grifón*. It is probably Scandinavian in origin. The remaining obsolete wrought-iron gun and associated breech-blocks were recovered from the same wreck. (Dr Colin Martin)

proved singularly slow. It was soon discovered that many of the ships' provisions were bad, and the Duke decided to put into the north-western Spanish port of La Coruña to repair his ships and restock the fleet's provisions. On 19 June the flagship and the leading ships entered La Coruña, but a sudden south-westerly gale scattered the rest throughout the Bay of Biscay. Medina Sidonia considered abandoning the enterprise, but the King ordered him to continue. The ships made their way into the port, the Duke supervised their repair, and within a month the Armada was once again ready to put to sea.

Medina Sidonia sailed from La Coruña on 21 July, and morale was reportedly high among the crews. Four days later he sent a pinnace ahead to warn Parma of his approach, and a brisk southerly breeze carried the rest of his fleet north towards England. The rough seas in the Bay of Biscay proved too much for the four galleys which accompanied the Armada, and they were forced to run for shelter to a French port. This was a serious blow, as they would have been vital support vessels during the landing in Kent. The *Santa Ana*, flagship of the Biscay Squadron, was also forced to drop out, having lost a mast. A week after leaving La Coruña the rest of the Armada was off Ushant (the western tip of Brittany) and the English coastline lay just beyond the northern horizon. Neither side knew it, but the rival fleets were only 100 miles apart.

A pocket map of the Bay of Biscay and the English Channel, reputedly belonging to Sir Francis Drake. Cartography was in its infancy, and errors caused problems for both sides during the campaign. (NMM, London)

OFF PLYMOUTH (30-31 JULY)

It was 1600hrs on Friday 29 July 1588 and 125 ships of various sizes stretched in a ragged line across three miles of ocean. As the flagship hoisted a flag bearing the Virgin Mary and a cross, the

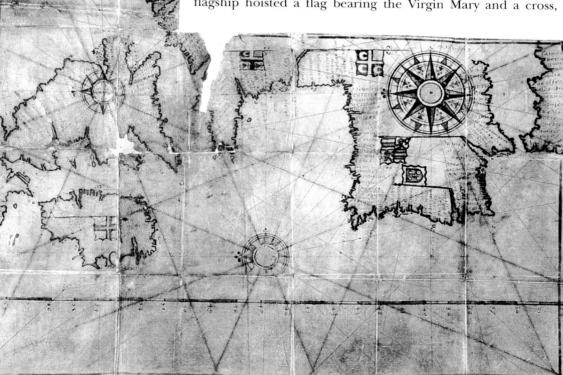

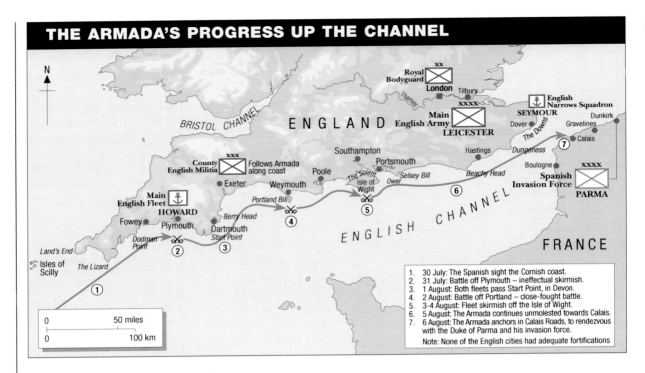

1. 30 July: The Spanish sight the Cornish coast.
2. 31 July: Battle off Plymouth – ineffectual skirmish.
3. 1 August: Both fleets pass Start Point, in Devon.
4. 2 August: Battle off Portland – close-fought battle.
5. 3-4 August: Fleet skirmish off the Isle of Wight.
6. 5 August: The Armada continues unmolested towards Calais.
7. 6 August: The Armada anchors in Calais Roads, to rendezvous with the Duke of Parma and his invasion force.

Note: None of the English cities had adequate fortifications

The Spanish Armada spent a week sailing up the English Channel, maintaining a tight defensive formation throughout the passage. For almost all that week the prevailing wind was a light westerly breeze, which favoured the Spanish. It also prevented any easy return passage from the Flemish coast once the Armada had rendezvoused with the Duke of Parma. The English fleet under Lord Howard gained the weather gauge on 31 July, and maintained that advantage throughout the campaign.

sailors gathered to hear mass. The Spanish Armada's crewmen had just sighted the Lizard, marking the start of the English coastline. The Duke of Medina Sidonia allowed the sailors to pray, then he ordered his ships to heave to and called his senior commanders together for a council of war. It would be the last chance to confer before the fighting started. The Duke's council included his Chief-of-Staff, Diego Flores de Valdés, the Deputy Armada Commander Juan Martinez de Recalde, six squadron commanders and Don Francisco de Bobadilla, commander of the embarked Spanish troops. Also present was a volunteer, Don Alonso de Leiva, charged with secret orders to take command of the Armada in the event of the Duke's death. While King Philip of Spain demanded that the Armada maintain a defensive formation as it travelled up the English Channel towards the Flemish coast, some of the commanders argued for a more aggressive approach.

Both De Leiva and Recalde proposed a direct assault on Plymouth, the main gathering point of the English fleet. If the English could be confined in the narrow harbour by part of the Spanish fleet, the rest of the Armada could sail down the Channel unimpeded. The Duke rejected the plan, emphasising that the Spanish objective was to reach Flanders, not become embroiled in a direct attack on the English fleet. He also made the last arrangements to his order of battle: Don Alonso would command the vanguard (consisting of the Levant and Guipúzcoa squadrons); Juan Martinez would lead the rearguard (the Biscay and Andalusia squadrons), and the Duke himself would control the main body or centre. He emphasised the importance of maintaining a tight defensive formation, and created a 'van'; a powerful ad-hoc squadron which could act as a 'fire-brigade'. It could race to support any portion of the defensive formation that was threatened by the English. The commanders returned to their ships, and the Armada was readied for battle.

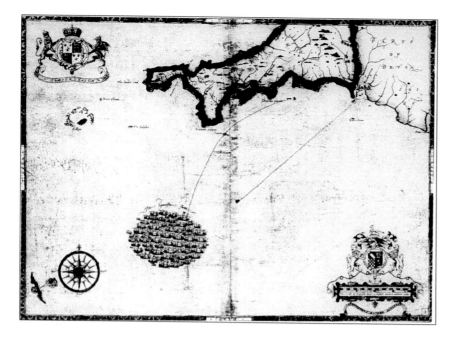

The Spanish Armada off the coast of Cornwall (29 July 1588). The chart shows the track of the Falmouth vessel which first spotted the Spanish fleet then raced back to Plymouth with the news. Chart 1 in a series of coloured engravings from *Expeditionis Hispnorum in Angliam vera description anno 1588*, by Robert Adams, 1590. (NMM)

By the next morning the Armada was sailing north-eastwards, following the line of the Cornish coastline for some dozen or so miles. Along the coast beacons were lit, a string of signals that stretched the length of the south coast. The news of the Armada's arrival had already reached Lord Howard in Plymouth because the previous night a scouting ship (probably the *Golden Hinde*) had caught sight of the Spanish fleet through Friday's rain squalls and raced into Falmouth with the news. That evening Howard and Drake managed to warp 54 ships out of Plymouth harbour; an impressive display of seamanship in the face of contrary winds and tides. Throughout Saturday morning the rest of the English fleet cleared the tricky entrance to Plymouth Sound, and the growing number of ships gathered off the Eddystone Rocks, some ten miles south of the harbour.

Howard planned to split his force into two: a main body and an inshore squadron. They would pass on either side of the Armada and rendezvous to the west of the Spaniards. This would give the English the weather gauge*. During the Spanish Armada campaign, the English held the weather gauge for most of the week-long fight up the English Channel. When the wind briefly shifted and gave the Spanish this advantage, Medina Sidonia tried to close with the English fleet off Portland (2 August), preventing the Spanish from attacking and gaining them the tactical initiative, allowing the English to dictate the course and pace of the action. The Armada would have been in sight by 1500hrs, but rain squalls hid the two fleets. During the afternoon the Spanish deployed from 'line of march' into 'line of battle', spreading into a crescent formation, with Recalde's rearguard on the left wing and De Leiva's vanguard on the right. They reduced sail during the night to prevent straggling. This also allowed the two sections of the English fleet to sail past the Armada on either side (north and south).

(NB: Throughout most of the narrative, the left wing of the Armada was opposite the left wing of the English fleet: the Armada was essentially

*The weather gauge
When manoeuvring for position, it was customary for sailing fleets to try to gain the weather gauge. This meant being to windward (or upwind) of the enemy. The enemy would find it very slow and difficult to sail upwind, but the fleet with the weather gauge could easily sail downwind towards the enemy. In other words, by holding the weather gauge, the windward fleet could dictate when and if battle was to be fought. Naturally, the fleet to leeward (downwind) could also avoid battle by simply running away.

Having the weather gauge also had advantages on the purely tactical level. The most significant of these being that when the wind caught the sails of the ship to leeward, it heeled over, exposing her hull below the waterline. Any shot hitting her exposed bottom could cause extensive flooding, and the ship could founder. The ship holding the weather gauge also had the advantage that her guns would recoil less because of the slope of the deck, and that smoke would blow clear of her guns.

The English warship *Griffin*, a privately owned armed merchant vessel of 200 tons. She is typical of the dozens of smaller vessels which formed the bulk of the English fleet. Engraving by Claes Jansz. Vissher. (NMM, London – 8.33)

fighting a rearguard action, and both fleets travelled in the same direction).

During the night a small Spanish scouting vessel captured a Falmouth fishing boat. Once the crew had been interrogated it became apparent that the English knew of the Spanish presence and there was no possibility of surprise. The English were at sea, and the following day would bring about the first battle of the campaign.

During the night the wind veered slightly, blowing west-north-west. The sea was also becoming rougher, and the rain squalls continued to pass up the Channel. At dawn, lookouts in the Armada saw the English ships to the south-west. Both the inshore and main squadrons had passed the Spaniards during the night and were taking up a position to windward, although the smaller inshore wing was still tacking westward to join Howard and the main body.

Medina Sidonia ordered his hulks to form into three groups ahead of the main fleet, protecting his supply vessels with the rest of his fleet. To the English the Armada must have been an imposing sight. One observer reported the Spanish ships deployed 'like a half-moon, the wings thereof spread out … sailing very slowly, with full sails … and the ocean groaning under their weight'.

Howard was accompanied by the small 80-ton bark *Distain*, and he ordered it to sweep down towards the centre of the Spanish formation and to fire an opening shot at the Spanish flagship. The 'flagship' turned out to be De Leiva's *La Rata Santa María Encoronada*, but the ceremonial shot prompted Medina Sidonia to unfurl his command flag on the real flagship, the *San Martín*. It was shortly after 0900hrs and the battle had begun.

Howard led his fleet in an attack on the centre and rear of the Spanish formation. Spanish witnesses describe the English attack as being '*en ala*', or 'in file' (line astern). This in itself was unusual, as ships usually fought by '*caracole*', firing a broadside, then turning to fire the other, then retiring to reload, firing the stern guns in the process. The cycle would then be repeated. With so many ships under his command, it made sense for Howard to order the rest of the fleet to follow him. In effect he was writing a manual for naval warfare as he went along. At the same time a handful of latecomers to the inshore squadron tacked within range of the Armada's northerly (left) wing. Two parts of the Armada formation were therefore under attack, the 'van' guarding the centre rear and the extreme tip of the left wing, a position held by the Squadron of Biscay, 'the windermost ships', as Sir Walter Raleigh described them.

When the Squadron of Biscay came under attack, most of the naos instinctively veered away from the enemy, closing in on the Squadron of Andalusia to starboard. This crowding left the two most northern ships exposed, Recalde's *San Juan de Portugal* and the *almiranta* (vice-flagship), *Gran Grin*. By this time more of the English inshore squadron were firing on the Spanish, with most of the shots being concentrated on the two naos. The records are unclear, but it has been suggested that Drake commanded the inshore squadron. Drake is also mentioned leading a

Detail of *The English and Spanish fleets engaged*, 1588. Oil painting, English School, late 16th century. The artist has included a wide range of Armada vessels of both sides and of various sizes, from galleons to small patches. In this depiction (probably representing the Battle off Gravelines), a Spanish galleon is shown foundering, with a priest swimming away from the wreck. (NMM – BHC0262)

The *San Salvador* exploding during the Battle off Plymouth (31 July 1588). Detail from *The English and Spanish fleets off Berry Head*, one of a series of engravings of the House of Lords Armada Tapestries, which were destroyed by fire in 1834. Engraving by John Pine, c.1739. The next day the captured vessel was towed into Weymouth, still smelling of charred timber and flesh. (NMM)

detachment of eight ships against Recalde, including Frobisher's and Hawkins' ships, which presumably formed part of the main body. Whoever commanded the attack, the fire was largely ineffective, since Spanish accounts mention that only 15 men were killed on Recalde's flagship that afternoon. As Howard's main battle line passed the Spanish 'van' they fired in succession at long range (about 500 yards), then continued north towards Recalde's wing. Witnesses in Plymouth describe hearing the sound of the guns in the distance and seeing the mass of ships and smoke on the horizon as the action slowly passed by, at a steady three or four knots.

Medina Sidonia saw the danger of having the enemy concentrate its force against his left wing so he ordered the 'van' to turn to port and steer north on a course parallel to the English. Don Alonso de Leiva, in *La Rata Santa María Encoronada*, took charge of the 'van' (abandoning his supervision of the unengaged right wing) and accompanied by the *San Mateo*, two other galleons and the galleasses, he tried to close with Drake and his ad-hoc squadron of eight vessels.

The English sea dog kept his distance and veered to port, avoiding becoming trapped between the powerful 'van' and the left wing of the crescent-shaped Spanish formation. Once the Spanish 'van' reached

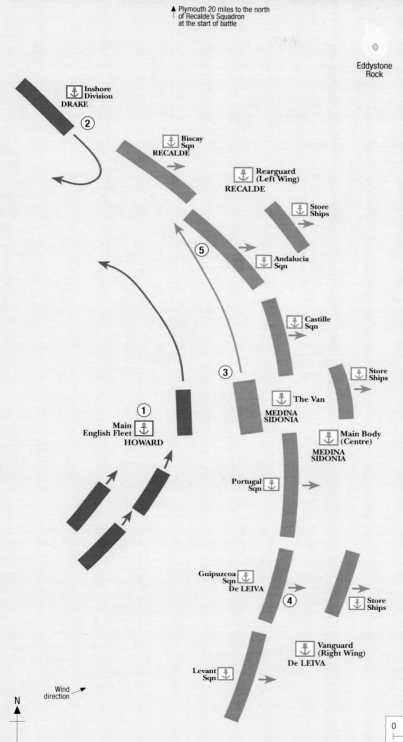

▲ Plymouth 20 miles to the north
of Recalde's Squadron
at the start of battle

Eddystone Rock

Inshore Division
DRAKE

②

Biscay Sqn
RECALDE

Rearguard (Left Wing)
RECALDE

Store Ships

⑤

Andalucia Sqn

Castille Sqn

Store Ships

③

The Van
MEDINA SIDONIA

Main English Fleet
HOWARD

①

Main Body (Centre)
MEDINA SIDONIA

Portugal Sqn

Guipuzcoa Sqn
De LEIVA

④

Store Ships

Vanguard (Right Wing)
De LEIVA

Levant Sqn

Wind direction

N

1. Phase 1 09:00 Charles Howard leads the attack of the main English fleet, dropping down from windward against the centre of the Spanish rearguard. The first shots were fired by the *Distain*, a small English pinnace. A general bombardment followed, but at 500 yards the range was too great to cause any real damage to the Spanish fleet. The Spanish rear was protected by a 'van' consisting of the four galleasses and a 'fire-brigade' of powerful galleons, commanded by Don Alonzo Martinez de Leiva.

2. Phase 2 10:30 A small English squadron had crept westwards, to the north of the Armada, and by mid-morning they were in position to windward of the Armada's right wing (rearguard), commanded by Juan Martinez de Recalde. They were probably commanded by Sir Francis Drake, and during the morning the squadron kept up a harassing fire against Recalde's Biscay Squadron. While many of the rest of his rearguard crowded in towards the centre of the Armada formation, Recalde in the *San Juan* and one other galleon took the brunt of the attacks. By noon they appeared perilously exposed.

3. Phase 3 12:00 The Spanish 'van' sails to support Recalde. According to an observer De Leiva in *La Rata Santa María Encoronada* got close enough to try to board Drake's *Revenge*, but the English 'sea-dog' kept his distance. The fighting soon died down, with both sides reduced to firing ineffectual long-range shots at the enemy.

4. Phase 4 13:30 An unexplained accident caused an explosion on board the *San Salvador* (958 tons), a galleon of the Guipuzcoa Squadron. It destroyed most of the vessel's stern castle, killing and wounding hundreds of Spanish seamen and soldiers. The Duke of Medina Sidonia ordered the ships of his right wing (vanguard) to support the crippled ship, and even ordered the entire Armada to heave to while this was carried out.

5. Phase 5 16:00 One of the 'fire-brigade' ships supporting Recalde was *Nuestra Señora del Rosario*, flagship of the Andalusia Squadron. Commanded by Don Pedro de Valdés it collided with another ship causing damage to the flagship's bowsprit. This made the galleon difficult to manoeuvre, and 30 minutes later it collided with another vessel, which brought down the foremast. Attempts to tow the *Rosario* were thwarted by the rising swell. The Armada commander ordered his fleet to regroup, and left the *Rosario* to its own devices. When the rest of the Armada altered course to the north-east around 18:00, the *Rosario* gradually fell behind the fleet, a vulnerable and tempting prize, drifting east down the Channel.

Note: Although Eddystone Rocks and Plymouth, located 20 miles away, are accurate for the start of the battle (approximately 9am), the engagement lasted for over seven hours and although the fleets retained the same relative positions in relation to each other, they moved steadily east at around five nautical miles an hour. By 4pm Plymouth was approximately 40 miles away from the centre of the battle bearing WNW.

0		1,000 yds
	1 nautical mile	
0		1,000 m

Recalde the crisis had passed, and the English were content to keep their distance, firing from windward at long range. The captain of the English ship *Bark Talbot* spoke of 'the majesty of the enemy's fleet' and 'the good order they held', while Howard later wrote of the battle: 'We durst not adventure to be put in amongst them, their fleet being so strong.' In other words, the English were unable or unwilling to close within effective range of the Armada's powerful defensive formation.

As the main battle was being fought around the Spanish wing, an unexpected disaster struck the Spanish in the vanguard, or right wing. Around 1330hrs a huge explosion ripped the sterncastle and part of the after decks out of the *San Salvador*, a large nao of the Squadron of Guipúzcoa. Although the exact cause remains unknown, it is probable that a powder barrel on the sterncastle exploded, setting off other powder barrels nearby. The blast killed or wounded hundreds of her crew and wrecked the vessel's steering mechanism. Medina Sidonia instantly ordered the Armada to heave to, and neighbouring ships came to the *San Salvador*'s aid, including the fleet flagship. Survivors were plucked from the water, and the fires on the *San Salvador* were extinguished while the wounded were transferred to other ships. By late afternoon the burnt and limping vessel was under way, escorted by the rest of her squadron.

Around 1600hrs a second disaster befell the Armada. One of the principal warships on the left wing was the *Nuestra Señora del Rosario*, the capitana of the Squadron of Andalusia, commanded by Don Pedro de Valdés. The neat formation of the Armada was disrupted as the 'van' and the two left wing squadrons crowded together. In the confusion Don Pedro's nao collided with a ship of the Squadron of Biscay and damaged her bowsprit. This affected the steering of the ship, and while repairs were being carried out the *Rosario* collided again, this time with the *Santa Catalina* of her own squadron. This second collision brought down her foremast. The sea was becoming rougher all the time, so Don Pedro sent a small ship to Medina Sidonia to ask for help. His ship was now virtually unmanoeuvrable. Counselled by Don Pedro's cousin Diego Flores de Valdés, Medina Sidonia decided that to rescue the *Rosario* would be to place the Armada in jeopardy. Don Pedro was abandoned and the *Rosario* drifted off to the east, while the rest of the Armada altered course slightly to the north-east.

Dusk and increasingly rough seas brought the first day's action to a close. While the Spanish had two ships damaged, neither was as a result of English attack. The defensive tactics of the Armada had been tested and

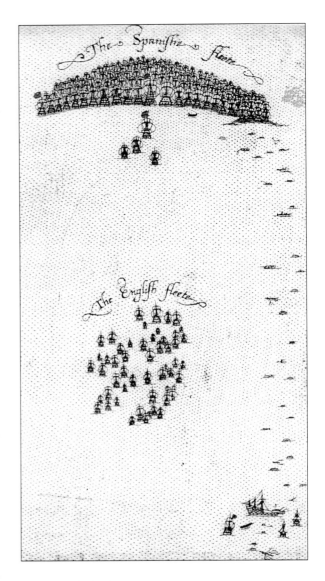

The capture of the *Nuestra Señora del Rosario* by Drake (bottom right), while the main English fleet pursues the Spanish Armada, defended by a rearguard surrounding the crippled *San Salvador* (dawn, 1 August 1588). Detail from Chart 4 in a series of coloured engravings from *Expeditionis Hispnorum in Angliam vera description anno 1588*, by Robert Adams, 1590. (NMM)

proven, and the integrity of her formation had never been seriously threatened.

Drake was ordered to shadow the Armada while the rest of the English fleet regrouped then followed on behind. This was presumably because following the English fleet's experiment with line ahead tactics, Drake was closest to the enemy. Howard sent a pinnace with orders that Drake was to light his stern lanterns to serve as a guide for the other ships. At around 2100hrs a small armed merchant vessel probed the wounded *Rosario* and was driven off by artillery fire. Drake was aware of the Spanish ship's plight and of her position. Instead of following the main fleet, he quietly altered course to starboard and shadowed the *Rosario* for the rest of the night.

Without their guide, Howard in the *Ark Royal* followed by the *Mary Rose* and the *White Bear* tried to shadow the Armada in the darkness, but the rest of the fleet lagged behind. In the mounting seas, the English ships became scattered in the darkness. Drake has been roundly criticised for his action, which placed his own desire for plunder before the needs of his nation, but he had built his reputation on privateering and would simply have found the opportunity too good to resist. Although he later claimed that he was pursuing strange sails and that he forgot to light his stern lantern, there is little doubt of his true actions or motives.

OFF DARTMOUTH (1 AUGUST)

Dawn on Monday 1 August found the Armada some 20 miles to the south of Start Point, and although still in its defensive formation, the fleet had become somewhat straggled during the night. The English were in a far worse position, as only Howard in the *Ark Royal* and his two consorts remained in position behind the Spanish and to windward. The English commander spent most of the morning hove to, waiting for his scattered fleet to gather around him, while the Armada a few miles away used the respite to heave to themselves, allowing Medina Sidonia time to reorganise its formation. With Don Pedro de Valdés and the *Rosario* lost somewhere to the south, his deputy, Don Diego Enríquez, became the new commander of the Squadron of Andalusia.

The problem with the horned or crescent-shaped defensive formation of the previous day was that it was cumbersome, and the extreme tips of the crescent had been vulnerable to attack. Medina Sidonia expected the English to bar his progress down the Channel, and his formation was perfectly designed to envelop and surround the smaller English fleet. Since the English ships kept the weather gauge and refused to allow the Spaniards to come near enough to board them, a new approach was needed. The Duke's solution was to join the horns together, forming a defensive circle rather than a crescent. Like the tercio formation used on land, the main body would be surrounded by smaller units. On land these would be musketeers, but at sea Medina Sidonia used his most powerful and well-armed ships, supported by his galleasses, which could tow the sailing warships if the wind failed. While Recalde busied himself with repairs to his flagship, Don Alonso de Leiva in *La Rata Santa María Encoronada* commanded the rearguard and the Duke controlled the main body of the fleet. The formation was partly a

OVERLEAF
DRAKE'S PURSUIT
OF THE *ROSARIO*
During the first battle of the campaign off Plymouth (31 July), the *Nuestra Señora del Rosario* served as the flagship of Don Pedro de Valdés, commander of the Andalusia Squadron. She damaged her bowsprit and foremast in the fight, and she fell behind the main Armada formation. By dusk she was well to the south of the Spanish fleet, which had changed course to the north-east.
Sir Francis Drake in the *Revenge* was ordered to shadow the Armada during the night, showing his stern lantern so the English fleet could follow him. Instead he extinguished all lights and headed south to intercept Don Pedro. The Englishman, who had made his name as a privateer, claimed he forgot about the lantern and that on seeing strange sails to the south he pursued them. At dawn he was two to three cables to windward of the *Rosario*. As Frobisher later retorted, this was because 'you were within two or three cables length ... all night!' Don Pedro duly surrendered to Drake, and the rich prize was towed into Falmouth. While the incident made the English privateer a rich man, it did little to further the English cause in the campaign, and amounted to a gross dereliction of duty. The plate shows Drake abandoning the Armada during the night, and setting course for the crippled *Rosario*.

The English and Spanish fleets off Berry Head, Devon, and the capture of the damaged Spanish galleon *San Salvador* (1 August 1588). While the Armada is shown in a tight defensive formation, the English fleet is straggling, racing to regain contact with the Spanish after Drake's sortie after the *Rosario*. Detail from Chart 5 in a series of coloured engravings from *Expeditionis Hispnorum in Angliam vera description anno 1588*, by Robert Adams, 1590. (NMM)

LEFT **Drake's capture of the** *Nuestra Senora del Rosario* (1 August 1588). Detail from *The English pursue the Spanish fleet east of Plymouth*, one of a series of engravings of the House of Lords Armada Tapestries, which were destroyed by fire in 1834. Engraving by John Pine, c.1739. (NMM)

response to the 'flinching' under fire, which had threatened to disrupt the Armada's defensive formation the day before. To avoid a repetition of this, Medina Sidonia sent small boats throughout the fleet, threatening that any captain who broke formation would suffer death by hanging. An executioner and provost marshal in each boat helped to emphasise the threat.

Further to the south, dawn found Don Pedro de Valdés and the *Rosario* alone but for one other ship, which was accompanied by a few small escorts. During the night Drake in the *Revenge* had shadowed the damaged galleon, and as the sun rose the sea dog was less than 500 yards to windward. He later expressed surprise at finding the *Rosario* at first light, prompting the sceptical Frobisher to comment: 'Ay marry, you were within two or three cables length [at dawn, as] you were no further off all night.' Although Drake could make excuses to his queen and his fleet commander, his fellow sea dogs and privateers knew exactly what his motives were.

The *Rosario* was virtually defenceless, since the *Revenge* could rake the Spanish vessel at will. Drake called on Don Pedro to surrender, and after an initial refusal the Spanish commander agreed to discuss terms with Drake on board the *Revenge*. After some contemplation, Don Pedro agreed to surrender his ship. The *Rosario* carried part of the Armada's pay chest – 50,000 gold ducats (or escudos), and the personal wealth of the ship's officers probably amounted to as much again. Although Drake was usually careful to prevent personal looting, his critics claim that only a portion of the plunder was handed over to the Crown.

While the armed merchantman *Roebuck* towed the *Rosario* into Dartmouth (some accounts say Weymouth), Drake sailed north with his high-ranking prisoners and the plunder to rejoin the main battle. By that afternoon Drake had rejoined Howard, who met Don Pedro and expressed sympathy for his plight. Howard was probably less sympathetic towards his own vice-admiral, who had deserted his post in search of plunder.

The reorganisation complete, the Armada was slowly sailing north-east, past Dartmouth, Berry Head and the entrance to Torbay. The Spanish had already lost one powerful warship, and they were about to lose another. The rough seas of the previous night had made it impossible to repair the *San Salvador*, and in the morning it was clear that she was taking on water from the damaged stern. At 1100hrs Medina Sidonia ordered the crew and valuables to be transferred to other ships, and as she was holding up the rest of the fleet, with the English force gathering to windward, he then ordered her to be abandoned or sunk. Not all the injured crewmen could be recovered in time, and by mid-afternoon the nao was cast adrift, as the Armada resumed its slow progress to the east.

THE CAMPAIGN OFF DEVON AND CORNWALL

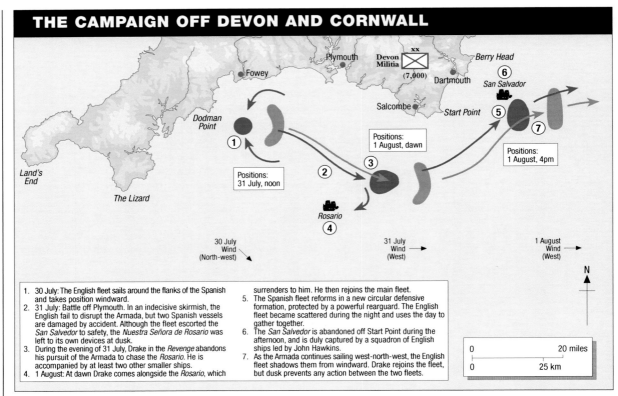

30 July Wind (North-west)

31 July Wind (West)

1 August Wind (West)

N

1. 30 July: The English fleet sails around the flanks of the Spanish and takes position windward.
2. 31 July: Battle off Plymouth. In an indecisive skirmish, the English fail to disrupt the Armada, but two Spanish vessels are damaged by accident. Although the fleet escorted the *San Salvedor* to safety, the *Nuestra Señora de Rosario* was left to its own devices at dusk.
3. During the evening of 31 July, Drake in the *Revenge* abandons his pursuit of the Armada to chase the *Rosario*. He is accompanied by at least two other smaller ships.
4. 1 August: At dawn Drake comes alongside the *Rosario*, which

surrenders to him. He then rejoins the main fleet.
5. The Spanish fleet reforms in a new circular defensive formation, protected by a powerful rearguard. The English fleet became scattered during the night and uses the day to gather together.
6. The *San Salvedor* is abandoned off Start Point during the afternoon, and is duly captured by a squadron of English ships led by John Hawkins.
7. As the Armada continues sailing west-north-west, the English fleet shadows them from windward. Drake rejoins the fleet, but dusk prevents any action between the two fleets.

0	20 miles
0	25 km

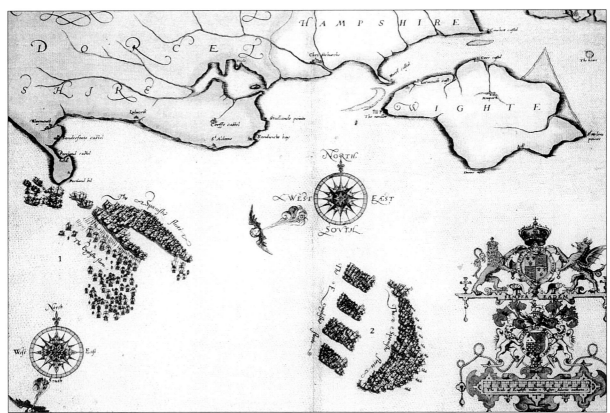

TOP, LEFT The Spanish sighted the Cornish coast on 30 July, although news of their coming had already reached Plymouth. Lord Howard put to sea that morning, and split his 150 ships into two groups; a small inshore squadron (probably commanded by Drake) and the main fleet. Both passed the Armada, and at dawn on 31 July they were to the west of the Spaniards, having gained the weather gauge. Although the resulting battle off Plymouth was little more than a skirmish, two Spanish ships were damaged; the *Nuestra Señora de Rosario* and the *San Salvador*. The *Rosario* was left behind by the rest of the Armada at dusk. During the night Drake in the *Revenge* accompanied by two small ships abandoned the pursuit of the Armada to shadow the *Rosario*. At dawn on 1 August he captured the Spanish warship, then returned to the north to rejoin Howard and the main fleet. Medina Sidonia decided to reorganise his fleet, placing the rearguard in the command of Don Alonso de Leiva. The English fleet had become badly scattered during the night, and was unable to organise an attack against the Armada, although the *San Salvador* was abandoned by the Spanish off Start Point and captured by the English. This first battle of the campaign had been indecisive, and the English were unable to break the tight defensive formation adopted by the Armada.

BOTTOM, LEFT The Battle off Portland and the Isle of Wight (2 and 3 August 1588). The confused fight off Portland is shown on the left, and following the failed attempt by the Spaniards to force the English into a close-range battle, the fleets continued sailing east-south-east. Chart 6 in a series of coloured engravings from *Expeditionis Hispnorum in Angliam vera description anno 1588*, by Robert Adams, 1590. (NMM)

Around 1600hrs John Hawkins in the *Victory* and Lord Thomas Howard in the *Golden Lion* came alongside the *San Salvador*. A witness described what they found: 'The deck of the ship had fallen down, the steerage broken, the stern blown out and about 50 poor creatures burnt with powder in most miserable sort. The stink in the ship was so unsavoury, and the sight within board so ugly, that Lord Thomas Howard and Sir John Hawkins shortly departed.' Thomas Flemyng in the small *Golden Hinde* took her under tow and eventually brought her into Weymouth.

Both fleets crept along within sight of each other during the late afternoon and early evening, but the wind had dropped to almost a whisper and progress was more with the tide than the wind. The rear of the Armada was protected by *La Rata*, the *Florencia*, the *San Mateo*, the *Santiago* and three of the galleasses, but the English never attempted to come within range. With the Armada maintaining a tight, powerful formation, the English were unable or unwilling to attempt any attack.

Howard preferred to bide his time and wait for an opportunity to attack on his own terms. He also remained unsure about the Armada's ultimate destination. Although Devon was safe, he could not rule out the possibility of a landing in Weymouth Bay or in the Solent. He needed to conserve his force for a battle to prevent any amphibious landing.

While the Armada was safe from any immediate English threat, Medina Sidonia was becoming increasingly concerned about his rendezvous with the Duke of Parma. He had no idea whether Parma was ready to embark his troops, or even whether Parma was aware that the Armada had sailed from La Coruña on 22 July. He therefore sent a Spanish officer (Juan Gil) in a fast pinnace with a message for Parma, outlining the events of the previous day and asking for pilots to help guide the Armada through the shoals which lay off the Flemish coast. 'Without them I am ignorant of the places where I can find shelter for ships so large as these, in case I should be overtaken by the slightest storm.' Gil was charged with arranging the union between Parma's invasion flotilla and the Armada, which was to protect the invasion barges. Medina Sidonia also changed the location of his rendezvous, from off Margate to Calais, where he would be able to form a tight protective ring around the barges for their short journey across the Channel.

OFF PORTLAND (2 AUGUST)

During the night the wind dropped completely, but shortly before dawn on Tuesday 2 August a breeze sprang up from the east-south-east. As the Spanish were to the east of the English fleet, this gave Medina Sidonia the advantage of the weather gauge for the first time, and he intended to use it to its best advantage. Howard was following the Armada on an easterly heading, and he immediately ordered his fleet to alter course and head north-north-east towards the coast. The Duke had already turned the Armada to port, and was heading on a north-north-westerly course, directly towards the peninsula of Portland Bill. For the first time the two fleets began to close with each other, and it looked as if the decisive encounter was about to take place. Within an hour it became

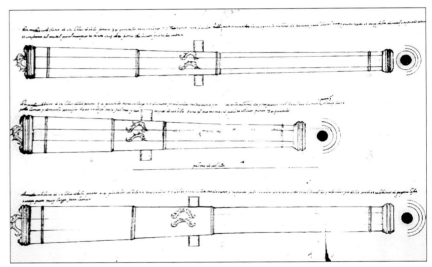

clear that the Spanish had won the race. Unable to creep between the Spanish and the shore to regain the weather gauge, Howard ordered his ships to come about and headed slowly to the south-south-west within four miles of the tip of Portland Bill.

The Armada had already formed into two distinct groups: the vanguard directly commanded by Medina Sidonia and a rearguard under Recalde, whose orders were to protect the supply ships and to support the vanguard if required. The vanguard was further divided into a 'van' consisting of the most powerful galleons, led by Martín de Bertendona of the Levant Squadron in *La Regazona*, and a main body led by Medina Sidonia in the *San Martín*. Howard's change of course gave Bertendona the opportunity to come to grips with the English fleet, and he turned his ships in a curve off the peninsula, mimicking the '*en ala*' tactics that had been used by his adversary off Plymouth two days before.

Avoiding the tidal rip off the peninsula known as the Portland Race, Howard's and Bertendona's squadrons converged at around 0900hrs. What

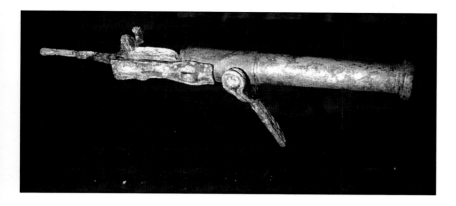

happened next is still unclear, but certainly for the first time the protagonists were within close range of each other; *La Regazona* and the *Ark Royal* were within musket range, as accounts mention small arms being used.

Behind Bertendona's flagship were the *San Mateo*, *La Rata Santa María Encoronada* and the *San Juan de Sicilia*. After an initial broadside, where the English 'stood fast and abode their coming', the *Ark Royal* turned to starboard, a change of course which was immediately followed by the other ships in the English line. In effect this was a simultaneous manoeuvre, presumably prompted by a pre-arranged signal, as the English fleet turned away from the enemy. This was part of the caracole manoeuvre, and although the English presented their sterns to the enemy, they prevented the Spanish from bringing on the boarding action they longed for.

The English probably continued to fire on the Spanish from a distance, and records indicate that Howard's flagship was accompanied by the *Victory*, the *Elizabeth Jonas*, the *Nonpareil* 'and divers others'. The Spanish 'were content to fall astern of the *Nonpareil*, which was the sternmost ship'. The firefight was therefore confined to a single close-range broadside, followed by sporadic fire at longer range, with the exchange continuing until around 1000hrs.

While the main body of the English fleet managed to avoid a close-range mêlée and boarding, another smaller part of the fleet found itself in grave danger. When the fleet had given up its attempt to cut between the Spanish Armada and the land, the six most leeward (inshore) ships had found themselves boxed in by Portland Bill and the Portland Race, unable to attempt to join the main fleet until the wind changed direction or freshened. The isolated group consisted of Martin Frobisher's *Triumph*, the warships *Golden Lion* and *Mary Rose* and the armed merchant vessels *Merchant Royal*, *Margaret and John* and *Centurion*. Frobisher later claimed his whole plan had been to lure a portion of the Spanish fleet into the shoals and tidal rips found off Portland, but he was more probably 'in distress', as Howard recounted after the battle.

The 'van' of the Spanish Armada led by Bertendona was already too far to the south to attack this isolated group, as was the main body of the fleet under Medina Sidonia. Further to the east, off the tip of Portland Bill, lay the Galleass Squadron commanded by Don Hugo de Moncada. Since the wind was dropping steadily, these four oared vessels were ideallly suited for the attack against Frobisher. Medina Sidonia sent a

The end of a Spanish linstock, recovered from the wreck of *La Trinidad Valencera*. It would be mounted on the end of a short hollow stick, and the burning slowmatch would stick through the mouth of the 'dragon'. (Dr Colin Martin)

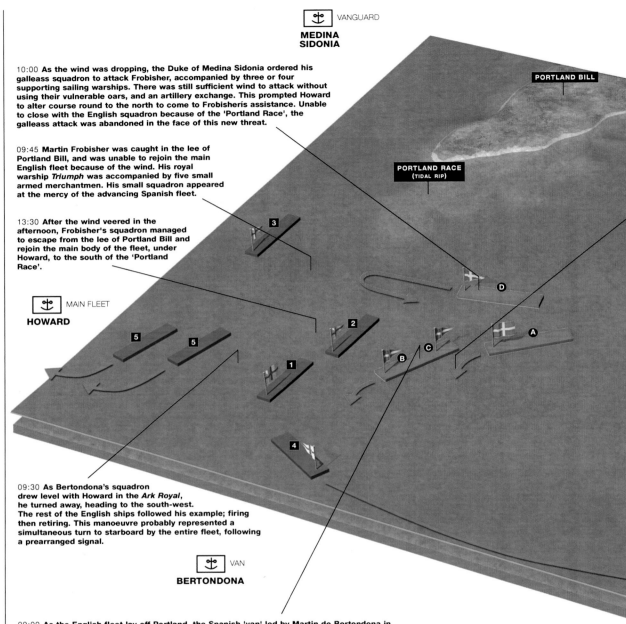

VANGUARD

MEDINA SIDONIA

10:00 As the wind was dropping, the Duke of Medina Sidonia ordered his galleass squadron to attack Frobisher, accompanied by three or four supporting sailing warships. There was still sufficient wind to attack without using their vulnerable oars, and an artillery exchange. This prompted Howard to alter course round to the north to come to Frobisher's assistance. Unable to close with the English squadron because of the 'Portland Race', the galleass attack was abandoned in the face of this new threat.

09:45 Martin Frobisher was caught in the lee of Portland Bill, and was unable to rejoin the main English fleet because of the wind. His royal warship *Triumph* was accompanied by five small armed merchantmen. His small squadron appeared at the mercy of the advancing Spanish fleet.

13:30 After the wind veered in the afternoon, Frobisher's squadron managed to escape from the lee of Portland Bill and rejoin the main body of the fleet, under Howard, to the south of the 'Portland Race'.

MAIN FLEET

HOWARD

PORTLAND BILL

PORTLAND RACE
(TIDAL RIP)

09:30 As Bertondona's squadron drew level with Howard in the *Ark Royal*, he turned away, heading to the south-west. The rest of the English ships followed his example; firing then retiring. This manoeuvre probably represented a simultaneous turn to starboard by the entire fleet, following a prearranged signal.

VAN

BERTONDONA

09:00 As the English fleet lay off Portland, the Spanish 'van' led by Martin de Bertondona in the *Regazona* turned to avoid the tidal anomaly known as the 'Portland Race'. They swept down on the English from the north-east, steering south-south-west. Both sides exchanged broadsides at close range.

BATTLE OF PORTLAND BILL (MEDINA SIDONIA OFFERS BATTLE), 2 AUGUST, 1588

Viewed from the south, the relatively slow and limited manoeuvring which took place allows us to show the development of the battle in relation to Portland Bill, the nearest point of land. A change in the wind allowed the Duke of Medina Sidonia to gain the weather gauge, and he used the opportunity to try to force a close-range engagement on the English fleet.

Note: The times given here are estimates, as the participants kept no accurate records.

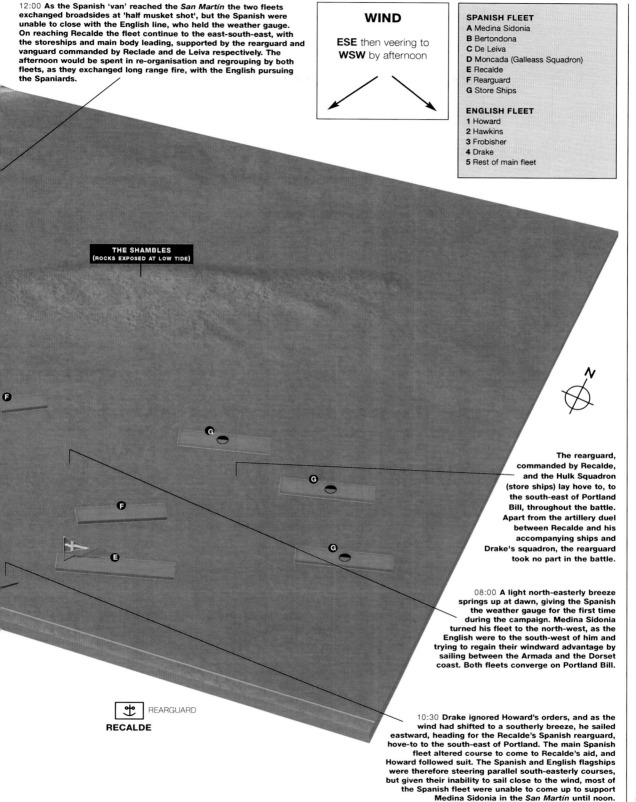

12:00 As the Spanish 'van' reached the *San Martín* the two fleets exchanged broadsides at 'half musket shot', but the Spanish were unable to close with the English line, who held the weather gauge. On reaching Recalde the fleet continue to the east-south-east, with the storeships and main body leading, supported by the rearguard and vanguard commanded by Reclade and de Leiva respectively. The afternoon would be spent in re-organisation and regrouping by both fleets, as they exchanged long range fire, with the English pursuing the Spaniards.

WIND

ESE then veering to
WSW by afternoon

SPANISH FLEET
A Medina Sidonia
B Bertondona
C De Leiva
D Moncada (Galleass Squadron)
E Recalde
F Rearguard
G Store Ships

ENGLISH FLEET
1 Howard
2 Hawkins
3 Frobisher
4 Drake
5 Rest of main fleet

THE SHAMBLES
(ROCKS EXPOSED AT LOW TIDE)

N

The rearguard, commanded by Recalde, and the Hulk Squadron (store ships) lay hove to, to the south-east of Portland Bill, throughout the battle. Apart from the artillery duel between Recalde and his accompanying ships and Drake's squadron, the rearguard took no part in the battle.

08:00 A light north-easterly breeze springs up at dawn, giving the Spanish the weather gauge for the first time during the campaign. Medina Sidonia turned his fleet to the north-west, as the English were to the south-west of him and trying to regain their windward advantage by sailing between the Armada and the Dorset coast. Both fleets converge on Portland Bill.

10:30 Drake ignored Howard's orders, and as the wind had shifted to a southerly breeze, he sailed eastward, heading for the Recalde's Spanish rearguard, hove-to to the south-east of Portland. The main Spanish fleet altered course to come to Recalde's aid, and Howard followed suit. The Spanish and English flagships were therefore steering parallel south-easterly courses, but given their inability to sail close to the wind, most of the Spanish fleet were unable to come up to support Medina Sidonia in the *San Martín* until noon.

⚓ REARGUARD
RECALDE

pinnace to Moncada with orders to attack Frobisher using sails and oars, and commanded the closest three or four sailing warships to support the attack. The Duke had not considered the Portland Race in his calculations.

Moncada's galleasses came close enough to Frobisher to engage in an artillery duel, and 'assaulted them sharply'. The English ships used the light winds for defensive caracole tactics, while the Spanish crept forward as far as the tidal rip. The Portland Race was a patch of water where strong tides moved concurrently in opposite directions. The same natural phenomenon which pinned Frobisher against the lee of Portland Bill also protected his ships. Moncada's galleasses were unable to enter the rip without being dragged to the side, and their commander was too cautious to close with Frobisher using full oars, as they were vulnerable in combat. Using sails alone, he lacked the mobility to close with Frobisher. Medina Sidonia sent a tart message to his galleass commander, containing 'certain words which were not to his honour'. Just as the attack petered out, the wind changed. A mild southerly breeze sprang up, which gave Howard the chance to support Frobisher. Howard reversed course, turning the main body of his fleet to the north to rendezvous with the isolated contingent.

The change in wind also altered the tactical situation. The 'van' of the Armada under Medina Sidonia and Bertendona was strung out in a line on a roughly southerly course, heading away from Portland Bill. The change of wind would have forced them to alter course slightly to either the south-east or south-west, but it is almost impossible to reconstruct Bertendona's actions from this point on. Howard and the English fleet were some distance to the west, while Drake and a handful of ships were ahead of both Howard and the Spaniards. Recalde and the Spanish rearguard were hove to further to the east of Medina Sidonia, with a line of warships protecting the vulnerable supply hulks.

To the north and rear of Medina Sidonia the private fight between Frobisher and Moncada was just ending. Howard's change of course had presented him with the option of cutting between Portland Bill and the rear of the Armada's main body. This was risky since it would have placed him between the Armada and a lee shore, where his fleet could have been trapped. It could also have precipitated a decisive close-range engagement. Howard opted for the safer course, steering to the west of the Portland Race. He did encourage his commanders to close the range to Medina Sidonia's ships, and 'to go within musket shot of the enemy before they should discharge any one piece of ordnance'. Howard's ships engaged the rear of the Spanish 'van', but the English fleet had become badly disorganised and only part of the formation could come to grips with the enemy.

To the south, Drake appeared to be taking matters into his own hands. The change of wind had placed him slightly to windward of Medina Sidonia, and level with the southern tip of Recalde's rearguard further east. He ignored Howard's orders to alter course to the north and instead steered to the east, closing with Recalde's *San Juan de Portugal*. Drake's and Recalde's formations were fighting in isolation of the main battle, with the Spanish formation representing an inverted horseshoe and the English in an L-shaped formation around its outside.

As accounts are vague and often contradictory, this stage of the battle

A ceramic firepot – a form of hand-thrown incendiary weapon carried on Spanish warships. Originally it would have held pitch and other combustible material, and burning slowmatch cords would have been tied around its waist. Recovered from the wreck of *La Trinidad Valencera*. (Ulster Museum, Belfast)

A range of shot types recovered from an early 17th-century Spanish shipwreck. All these types of ammunition were used during the Armada campaign: stone shot (for 'perriers'), regular roundshot and 'dice shot' (for close-defence firing). (Mel Fisher Maritime Museum, Key West, FL)

remains difficult to follow in anything other than the broadest terms. Seeing that his rearguard was under threat, Medina Sidonia ordered several of his most powerful warships to sail to Recalde's support. In all probability this meant that the ships around Recalde at the rear of the 'van' were ordered to alter course to starboard and sail on an east-south-easterly heading. Bertendona's command probably remained in position to windward of the English fleet and waited for further orders. *La Rata Santa María Encoronada* is mentioned as coming to Recalde's aid, and earlier in the day Don Alonso de Leiva's ship was reported to have been following Bertendona's *Regazona*. It is probable that Don Alonso was simply acting on his own initiative, although he may have led a general regrouping of the 'van', bringing it round to form a tighter formation in support of Recalde. An English witness described the Spanish as flocking together like sheep. This probably meant they were tightening up their defensive formation after the failure of Bertendona's 'van' to bring the enemy to close quarters.

This left Medina Sidonia in the *San Martín* at the apex of the horseshoe formation, now rapidly becoming a circle. Howard realised that his opponent was exposed, and ordered part of his fleet to reverse course once again and head south-east towards the Spanish flagship. The Spanish were now subjected to a two-pronged attack, with a southerly group led by Drake attacking Recalde, and a north-westerly group under Howard attacking Medina Sidonia. At this stage both Howard and the Spanish 'van' were probably on a south-easterly heading, under light sail. Medina Sidonia even lowered his topsails, encouraging Howard to close and fight a boarding action, a chivalric gesture which Howard ignored.

The *Ark Royal* was followed in line astern by the *Elizabeth Jonas, Galleon Leicester, Golden Lion, Victory, Mary Rose, Dreadnought* and *Swallow*. Presumably the rest of the English fleet were further to the north-west and were bystanders to the action. The English advantage lay in gunnery, and their main fleet pounded the *San Martín* at 'half-musket shot', shrouding the Spanish ship in smoke. As one Spanish witness put it: 'The galleon *San Martín*, being to windward of the Armada and near the enemy's ships, the latter attacked her with the whole of their cannon, she returning the fire with so much gallantry that on one side alone she fired of hundred shots, and the enemy did not care to come to close quarters with her although she was alone, and her consorts were unable to aid her for one and a half hours.'

At some point in the early afternoon Don Alonso de Leiva and a 'fire brigade' of Spanish ships managed to work their way through their own fleet to support the flagship. Along with the *San Marcos* and the *Santa Ana*, Leiva screened the flagship and escorted it to the comparative safety of the main body of the Armada.

Deprived of their victim and faced by a solid line of powerful Spanish warships, the English altered course to the south-west, and headed out to sea to regroup, accompanied by the handful of ships around Frobisher. Further to the south, Drake gave up his half-hearted attack on Recalde's wing, presumably because Bertendona's 'van' had managed to come up to support the rearguard. After the fury of the morning and early afternoon, both sides retired to patch their vessels and to determine their next move.

The action centred on the *San Martín* had demonstrated the basic differences between the Spanish and English tactics. The Spanish flagship had made several attempts to board the English vessels, but the English had kept their distance. Both sides had fought a fierce artillery duel, but by almost all accounts the English had fired three shots for every one from the Spanish. This English advantage in gunnery came about through their adoption of four-wheeled truck carriages; the Spanish used larger two-wheeled sea carriages. The English carriages were easier to use, and allowed the guns to be reloaded at a faster rate. The Spanish also lashed their carriages to the side of the ship, while the English used a system of blocks and tackles to run their guns in and out and to hold them in position. This also meant that the English ships expended more powder and shot. Howard sent a messenger ashore with a request for more munitions, and he suggested removing powder from the two Spanish vessels captured the previous day. The effectiveness of the English fleet was temporarily reduced because of this lack of powder.

The damage inflicted by the English gunnery was surprisingly light. The *San Martín* had borne the brunt of the fighting, but although her hull had been pierced and her rigging cut up, the damage was largely superficial. The English had demonstrated their superiority in gunnery,

THE CAMPAIGN OFF DORSET AND HAMPSHIRE

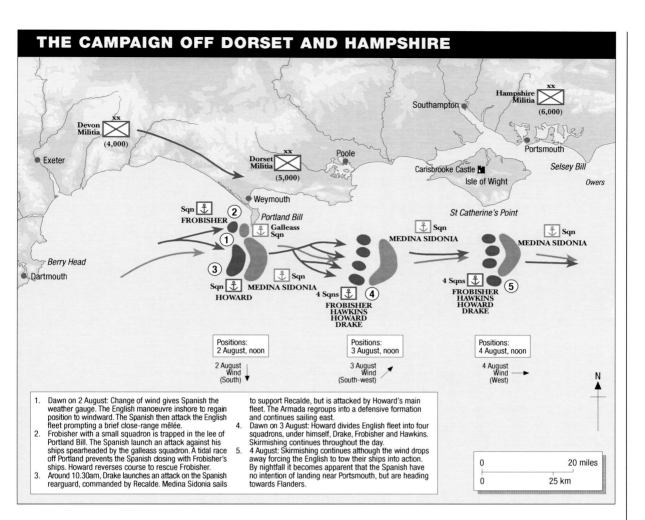

1. Dawn on 2 August: Change of wind gives Spanish the weather gauge. The English manoeuvre inshore to regain position to windward. The Spanish then attack the English fleet prompting a brief close-range mêlée.
2. Frobisher with a small squadron is trapped in the lee of Portland Bill. The Spanish launch an attack against his ships spearheaded by the galleass squadron. A tidal race off Portland prevents the Spanish closing with Frobisher's ships. Howard reverses course to rescue Frobisher.
3. Around 10.30am, Drake launches an attack on the Spanish rearguard, commanded by Recalde. Medina Sidonia sails

to support Recalde, but is attacked by Howard's main fleet. The Armada regroups into a defensive formation and continues sailing east.
4. Dawn on 3 August: Howard divides English fleet into four squadrons, under himself, Drake, Frobisher and Hawkins. Skirmishing continues throughout the day.
5. 4 August: Skirmishing continues although the wind drops away forcing the English to tow their ships into action. By nightfall it becomes apparent that the Spanish have no intention of landing near Portsmouth, but are heading towards Flanders.

but they had failed to harm the Armada, or to disrupt its formation. Total Spanish casualties for the battle were estimated at 50 men throughout the entire fleet, and English losses were minimal. As the English gunner William Thomas put it: 'What can be said but our sins was the cause that so much powder and shot (were) spent, and so long a time in (the) fight, and in comparison thereof, so little harm (done to the enemy)'.

Long-range skirmishing continued throughout the rest of the afternoon but neither side would be drawn into another major engagement. Howard and Drake both thought that Medina Sidonia's objective was the Isle of Wight, and with their powder stocks dangerously low, they felt they would be hard-pressed to prevent the Spanish landing troops on the island or entering the Solent. The Hampshire Militia stood to arms, and beacons flared along the coast.

For his part, Medina Sidonia was becoming increasingly concerned about his impending rendezvous with the Duke of Parma. Once past the Isle of Wight there was no safe anchorage for the Armada, and it would be committed to a rendezvous off Calais. Heading into the Solent would delay the campaign but it would also give Parma time to prepare his troops for embarkation.

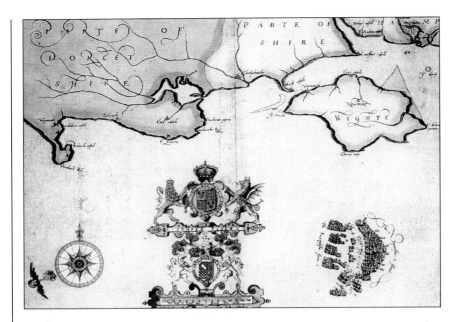

During the evening Medina Sidonia reorganised the Armada, and his orders reflected his new doctrine: 'The important thing for us is to proceed on our voyage, for these people do not mean fighting, but only to delay our progress.' Clearly the lack of effectiveness of the English gunnery had made him contemptuous of their ability to prevent him from reaching his objective. His new formation consisted of two fighting squadrons: the 'rearguard' commanded by Recalde and the 'vanguard' under De Leiva. These squadrons would protect the main body led by Medina Sidonia, which also protected the supply hulks. As night fell the wind changed once again, this time reverting to the westerly wind which had predominated during the previous few days. Both fleets were sailing east-south-east, with the English behind and to windward of the Spanish. The following day would determine whether the battle would be continued in the approaches of the Solent or whether the Armada would continue its progress down the Channel.

OFF THE ISLE OF WIGHT (3-4 AUGUST)

At dawn on Wednesday 3 August the English fleet pursuing the Armada noticed that one of the Spanish vessels had fallen behind the rest of the fleet, at the southern tip of the Armada formation. She was the *El Gran Grifón*, the flagship of Juan Gómez de Medina, commander of the squadron of hulks. Several English ships raced forward to attack her, led by Drake in the *Revenge*. Drake fired a broadside at close range, then raked the hulk and loosed a second broadside. The *Grifón* was struck by over 40 roundshot, but no serious damage was inflicted. Musket balls flattened by impact recovered in the 1970s from the wreck of the Spanish vessel, suggest that the combatants fought within range of small-arms fire. Although the *Revenge* and her consorts were able to outmanoeuvre the *Grifón* and batter her with gunfire, they could not to stop her. Medina Sidonia sent support for Juan Gómez; Don Hugo de Moncada and the

DVNNE.NOSE.

Battle off 'Dunne Nose' (St. Catherine's Point, Isle of Wight), from *The Armada's progress from Plymouth to Gravelines*. Engraving by Claes Jansz. Visscher. Although tactically inaccurate, the artist gives a good impression of the ships involved, and the way in which they fought. (NMM 8.34)

Galleass Squadron, with Recalde's rearguard at long range. The galleasses managed to tow the battered hulk of the *Grifón* back into the safety of the Armada's defensive formation, and then Recalde and De Leiva were ordered to close with the English ships and try to initiate another engagement. Instead the *Revenge* and her consorts withdrew, and the rest of the English fleet hove to well to windward of the Spanish, avoiding an engagement.

Howard's reluctance to fight was probably caused by his chronic lack of munitions. For the rest of the day the two fleets wallowed along in extremely light airs, and the Armada crept towards the Isle of Wight. As the day wore on it became apparent that Medina Sidonia had little intention of making for the western entrance of the Solent, but Howard still suspected that the Armada planned to anchor in the shelter of the eastern side of the Isle of Wight. That evening he called his senior commanders together on board the *Ark Royal*. It was decided that the English fleet should be reorganised into four squadrons, to be commanded by Howard, Drake, Hawkins and Frobisher. Instead of simply following the flagship, the new structure allowed the fleet to operate in smaller, more manoeuvrable formations. Howard stressed that the principal aim of any battle the following day was to prevent the Spanish from entering the Solent or attempting to land.

During the night two more Spanish ships dropped behind the Armada, and at dawn on Thursday 4 August the *San Luís* and the *Duquesna Santa Anna* lay between the two fleets. The wind had died away completely during the early hours and any attempt to attack the two Spanish stragglers would mean towing the English warships into range.

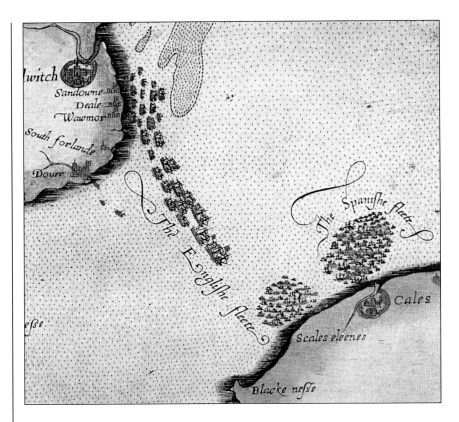

Hawkins' squadron was closest to the two ships, and he immediately ordered his ships to lower their boats. As the English were towing their ships into position, Recalde detached two galleasses to protect the stragglers; a third towed De Leiva's *La Rata Santa María Encoronada* to safety.

Hawkins' ships opened fire on the galleasses and, according to Hawkins, they managed to damage one of the three oared vessels. In turn Hawkins was forced to withdraw his boats when they were peppered by Spanish small-arms fire. The *Ark Royal* and the *Golden Lion* were towed into the fray, but the English were unable to prevent Moncada from rescuing the two Spanish ships. The three galleasses rejoined the Armada formation, each towing a sailing ship behind it.

By mid-morning a slight south-westerly breeze gave the English the weather gauge again, allowing Frobisher on the English left (northern) wing to run before the wind, placing his leading ships between the Armada and the eastern edge of the Solent. The *Triumph* fired on the *San Martín*, which had become isolated for the second time in as many days. The Spanish flagship was holed twice below the waterline before she could be escorted to safety. Several Armada ships were despatched to attack Frobisher, possibly the vanguard formation commanded by De Leiva himself. A freak of the wind deprived Frobisher of sail-power, while the Spanish to the south were still able to close the range. In desperation he lowered the *Triumph*'s boats and tried to tow his ship to safety. At the last minute his sails caught the wind and he escaped to the north.

Hawkins and Howard launched another attack against Recalde on the Armada's southern flank. A brisk engagement followed, and as one

Spaniard put it, 'If the Duke had not gone about with his flagship … we should have come out vanquished that day.' From this it seems that elements of the main body were forced to break formation and return to assist the rearguard commanded by Recalde. It has been argued that Drake led this attack, slowly working his unengaged squadron to seaward of the rest of the fleets, then, as they became engaged, he turned against De Leiva's flank. Whoever masterminded the attack, it succeeded in diverting the Spanish for two crucial hours. By the time the English fleet regrouped in mid-afternoon, Medina Sidonia had missed his opportunity to turn towards the Solent. He now had no option but to continue sailing down the Channel towards Calais. That night he sent another pinnace racing ahead with a message for the Duke of Parma.

If Medina Sidonia had planned to anchor in the Solent or off the eastern side of the Isle of Wight, he kept his plans to himself. His formation remained intact, and as the English drew back to a safe distance, the Armada was allowed to continue its progress down the Channel. Another boat was sent ahead to Dunkirk, this time asking for 40 to 50 small light craft to help harass the English fleet. For their part the English needed reinforcements and supplies if they were to continue the fight. Howard wrote: 'Forasmuch as our powder and shot was well wasted, the Lord Admiral thought it was not good in policy to assail them any more until their coming near unto Dover.'

After a rendezvous with Seymour and the squadron of supply ships sent from the Thames, Howard would continue the fight somewhere between Calais and the Kent coast. For all of the following day (5 August) the two fleets continued their progress, heading north-north-east towards the Straits of Dover in very light winds. In another meeting on board the English flagship, Howard knighted Hawkins and Frobisher for their services during the campaign.

At 1000hrs on Saturday 6 August the Armada came within sight of the French coast near Boulogne. It maintained a tight defensive formation and by the late afternoon had dropped anchor in Calais Roads. The Duke of Medina Sidonia had sailed the full length of the English Channel with his fleet relatively intact and its defensive integrity maintained. All that remained was to arrange a rendezvous with the Duke of Parma's troops at Dunkirk and to escort them across the Channel. Medina Sidonia held a council of war that evening, when it was decided to remain in the exposed anchorage off Calais until Parma's small fleet had joined the Armada. For their part the English anchored some miles to the west, maintaining their windward advantage. That evening Howard was joined by Seymour's squadron, bringing much-needed supplies and munitions from the Thames. The English fleet now numbered around 140 ships, but Howard planned to expend some of these vessels in order to break the tactical deadlock.

OFF CALAIS (7 AUGUST)

Late on Saturday night Howard sought the advice of Sir William Winter of the *Vanguard*, who reportedly suggested using fireships against the Spanish fleet. Howard was enamoured with the idea, and early the following morning he called his senior commanders together for a

An English 'race-built' galleon; a detail from *The launch of the English fireships against the Armada at Calais, 7 August, 1588.* Oil painting, Dutch school, c.1595. These modern English vessels were simply better armed and more manoeuvrable than their Spanish counterparts. (NMM – BHC0263)

council of war on board the *Ark Royal*. Seymour, Drake, Hawkins and Frobisher approved the plan, and its execution was set for midnight that night. Howard sent Sir Henry Palmer of the *Antelope* to Dover to commandeer suitable vessels and combustible materials. Seymour had already gathered a store of brushwood and pitch at Dover for exactly this purpose. The freshening south-westerly wind made their arrival before midnight unlikely, so Howard was forced to sacrifice vessels from his own fleet. After further consultation with his squadron commanders, eight armed merchantmen were selected for conversion into fireships.

The ships selected were the *Bark Talbot* and *Thomas Drake* (both of 200 tons), the *Hope of Plymouth* (180 tons), the *Bark Bond* and *Cure's Ship* (both of 150 tons), the *Bear Yonge* (140 tons), the small *Elizabeth of Lowestoft* (90 tons) and one other even smaller vessel. For the rest of the day carpenters worked on the vessels, strengthening rigging, altering or removing the gunports and possibly cutting exit ports in the stern for the skeleton crew to escape through. Other seamen gathered all the

combustible materials which could be found in the fleet (old sails, cordage, hemp, tar, pitch, etc.), and soaked the ships in oil. They also loaded and double-shotted the guns, so that when the heat ignited the charges, they would fire into the enemy fleet and increase the confusion. A handful of volunteers were selected to steer each ship towards the Armada. At the last moment the tiller or whipstaff would be lashed and the crew would escape over the stern into a waiting longboat which was towed behind each fireship.

THE FIRESHIP ATTACK AT CALAIS

During the morning of 7 August, Howard decided to launch a midnight fireship attack against the Spanish fleet at anchor off Calais. The English were to windward (upwind), so the fireships could be sailed straight towards the mass of Spanish shipping, aided by the flooding tide. Behind the Armada lay the treacherous sandbars of the Banks of Flanders. During the day English shipwrights converted eight small vessels for the attack, loading them with combustibles and powder.

Around midnight Spanish scout ships saw the fireships and raised the alarm. They managed to tow two of the fireships clear of the fleet, but the remainder continued unimpeded.

The Spanish commander ordered his ships to cut their anchors and escape to safety. Although no ships were damaged by the fireships, without their main anchors the Armada was unable to remain in position off Calais, and by dawn the fleet was disorganised and drifting to the north-east of Calais. It was now impossible for the Armada to rendezvous with the Duke of Parma's army. The plate shows the initial launch of the fireships; small English merchant vessels, seen from the west. In the distance the Armada is still at anchor in Calais Roads, its commanders unaware of the English attack.

The English fireships drift down on the Spanish fleet (7 August 1588). Detail from *The Fireship Attack*, one of a series of engravings of the House of Lords Armada Tapestries, which were destroyed by fire in 1834. Engraving by John Pine, c.1739. (NMM, London)

While the English were busy preparing for their night-time attack, the Duke of Medina Sidonia was trying to determine his next move. Although he had sent two messages to Parma as the Armada sailed up the Channel, he had not received any reply. On 2 August Parma was informed that the Armada had left La Coruña, but he only heard it was approaching Calais on 5 August, the day before the fleet anchored in Calais Roads. For the first time, the two commanders could communicate with each other. A messenger reported that the Duke of Parma was still at his headquarters in Bruges, and his troops and stores were still in their camps. They had not even started to board the invasion barges which would transport them to Kent. Meanwhile word also came of a Dutch coastal squadron blockading Dunkirk and Nieuport, making it difficult for Parma to put to sea. The barges would have to creep towards Gravelines using the Flemish network of small canals and rivers, and it was estimated that the process would take anything up to two weeks. Medina Sidonia's fleet was in an unsheltered anchorage off a neutral port, with a powerful English fleet to windward and the mass of sandbanks known as the Banks of Flanders to leeward. It was an unenviable position, but he had little option but to remain in place and wait for Parma.

The French Governor of Calais was Giraud de Mauleon, Seigneur de Gourdan. As a Catholic who had lost a leg fighting the English 30 years earlier, his sympathies lay with Spain. Presents were exchanged between the governor and Medina Sidonia, and a Spanish delegation went ashore to liaise with the French and buy provisions for the fleet. It was headed by the Duke of Ascoli, who also established firm lines of communication with Parma in Bruges. Throughout the day French boats ferried food and supplies out to the waiting Spanish ships, supervised by the Armada's paymaster-general, Don Jorge Manrique. That evening Don Jorge was ordered to ride to Bruges to persuade the Duke of Parma to speed up his embarkation.

During the evening the wind changed from the south-west to the west, the same direction as the tidal flow. That Sunday it was also a full moon, so the spring tides were at their strongest. Both the wind and the flood tide were therefore in the English favour, and as final preparations were made for the fireships, the rest of the fleet prepared for a naval attack on the Armada the following day. For his part Medina Sidonia placed a screen of light craft (*carvels, pataches, falúas* or *zabras*) to the west of his anchorage, between the Armada and the English fleet. Similar screening vessels were presumably deployed to the east, to prevent any surprise attack by the Dutch. Soon after midnight Spanish lookouts on these screening craft spotted two glowing ships heading towards them from the English fleet two miles away. What had happened was that the fireship attack had been launched on schedule, but on two of the eight vessels the fires had either been ignited prematurely or the vessels had proved particularly combustible. This gave the Spanish some advanced warning of the impending attack, and the alarm was raised.

To the Spanish, fireships had a particularly alarming association, since just over three years before, the Dutch rebels had launched an attack against a Spanish pontoon bridge across the River Schelde, near Antwerp. The Dutch fireships had been packed with explosives, and the resulting devastation destroyed the bridge and cost the lives of 800 Spanish soldiers. The Dutch engineer who had created them was known to have moved to England, and could well have been behind this attack.

In fact the English fireships were far less lethal and consequently far less effective. Around midnight the flood tide moved east at three knots, and although they carried minimal sails, the fireships would be among the Armada within 15 or 20 minutes. The small screening ships managed to grapple and tow two of the eight vessels out of the path of the Armada, but the other six were presumably blazing too fiercely to approach. Medina Sidonia reacted swiftly to the threat, and issued the only sensible order he could. Pinnaces were sent through the fleet ordering the ships to cut their anchor cables, raise their sails and escape to seaward. He hoped that once the threat had passed, the Armada would be able to regroup and anchor in the same position again.

Subsequent English accounts have suggested that the Spanish panicked and fled, but this has since been refuted. Like almost all evolutions undertaken by the Armada, it was a seamanlike manoeuvre, accomplished with almost complete success. Of the mass of craft that made up the fleet, only one vessel collided with another in the darkness. The galleass *San Lorenzo* broke her rudder in the collision and spent the night trying to creep back towards Calais under oars. The remainder of the fleet avoided the fireships but were unable to regain their original anchorage in Calais Roads. The strong flood tide, combined with a seabed which provided poor holding meant that most of the ships were unable to anchor and they drifted to the north-east, towards Gravelines and the Banks of Flanders.

This turned out to be the single most decisive incident of the campaign. The Armada had been driven from its anchorage, and its ships had been forced to sacrifice their best and strongest anchors. These were irreplaceable, and the remaining smaller anchors would be unable to provide a purchase in the tidal waters off Calais. Although the Armada remained undamaged, it was scattered, and for the first time since the campaign began it was strung out over miles of sea; it had lost the tight defensive formation that had enabled it to cross the Channel in relative safety.

The loss of the anchorage also meant that the Armada was now unlikely to be able to rendezvous with the Duke of Parma. One English historian called the purchase of the eight fireships for just over £5,000 'the cheapest national investment the country has ever made'. It was also one of the most effective. The Spanish lay off some of the most dangerous coastal waters in Europe, and without anchors their position was precarious. Only five galleons managed to anchor in their original position, including Medina Sidonia's *San Martín* and Recalde's *San Juan de Portugal*. The rest of the Armada lay scattered in the darkness, and to windward the English fleet was preparing to fight the climactic battle of the campaign.

OFF GRAVELINES (8-9 AUGUST)

At dawn Medina Sidonia in the *San Martín* found himself accompanied by only four other galleons: the *San Juan de Portugal*, the *San Marcos*, the *San Juan Bautista* and the *San Mateo*. The English fleet moved in for the attack and Medina Sidonia fired his guns as a signal for the Armada to regroup for battle. It would take some considerable time before they would be able to re-establish their defensive formation, and in the meantime these five galleons were all that stood between the scattered fleet and the English. The battle began around 0700hrs and would last throughout the day, the most intensive and bloody action of the campaign.

The galleass *San Lorenzo*, which had damaged its rudder during the fireship attack, had grounded on a sandbar off Calais during the night. She was the almiranta of the Galleass Squadron, the flagship of Don Hugo de Moncada, and therefore was seen as too tempting a prize for the English to ignore. Howard himself led his squadron in an attack on the lone ship, leaving the rest of the fleet to engage Medina Sidonia.

The shoals prevented the English warships from coming in close, so ships' boats were used to attack the galleass, supported by long-range fire. The fighting was fierce for almost an hour, until Don Hugo was shot through the head with a musket ball. With their commander killed, the Spaniards lost heart and either surrendered or fled in boats towards the shore. The English sailors began to pillage the *San Lorenzo*, and while Bernabe de Pedroso (the senior Spanish officer in Calais) rallied the survivors, his appeals for French assistance were ignored. Eventually the Spaniards managed to drive off the English with small-arms fire (some accounts mention artillery, which is unlikely), but soon after the looters retreated, the French rowed out to plunder the vessel. When they were threatened by returning English seamen, the French reputedly threatened to fire on the English boats.

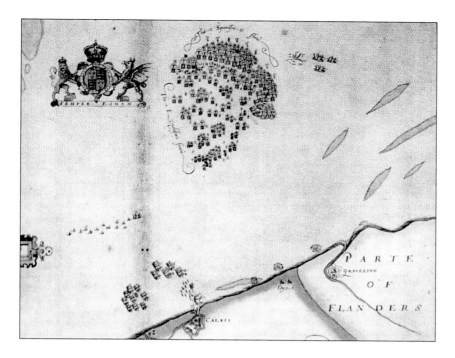

The Battle off Gravelines (8 August 1588). While part of the English fleet chases the disorganised Armada, other English ships are shown attacking the crippled galleass *San Lorenzo* off Calais. Chart 10 in a series of coloured engravings from *Expeditionis Hispnorum in Angliam vera description anno 1588*, by Robert Adams, 1590. (NMM)

The whole action lasted some two hours and diverted almost half of the English fleet from the initial phase of the main battle, which was raging to the north. Eventually the *San Lorenzo* was returned to the Spanish authorities, together with her armament of 50 guns. The armament was removed, but the galleass was abandoned where she lay. The whole incident benefited the Spanish, as it gave the Armada a brief respite to reorganise its defences.

Medina Sidonia decided to stand and fight with his five warships, buying time for the rest of his fleet to organise themselves into some kind of defensive formation. Presumably Don Alonso de Leiva was charged with this reorganisation, as both Medina Sidonia and Juan Martinez de Recalde were in the 'forlorn hope' or small blocking force facing half the English fleet. It seems that the Duke was willing to sacrifice his own ship and its consorts in order to save the rest of his fleet.

The *San Martín* withstood several hours of close-range fighting at 'half musket shot'. Drake in the *Revenge* led the first attack, an honour which would have been given to Howard had he not been preoccupied with the attack on the *San Lorenzo*. At one point the Spanish flagship was surrounded by Drake in the Revenge, Hawkins in the *Victory* and Frobisher in the *Triumph*, while other English ships lined up to take their turn. It was estimated that during the two-hour action the *San Martín* was hit over 200 times by roundshot. Her hull and rigging were badly damaged, her decks 'awash with blood'.

The other Spanish ships of the 'forlorn hope' fared almost as badly, but gradually they managed to creep northward to now rejoin the rest of the fleet, which by then had managed to form into some semblance of order. By 1000hrs the *San Martín* and her consorts were safely inside a ring of Spanish warships, and the English prepared themselves for an attack against the main body of the Armada. What followed would essentially be a running fight, with the Spanish trying to maintain a tight

defensive formation while striving to keep as close as possible to the Flemish coast. The English objective was to concentrate on attacking the wings of the formation using close-range fire, and to try to force the Armada onto the sandbanks to the east.

According to Sir William Winter in the *Vanguard*, the Armada 'went into a proportion of a half moon. Their admiral and vice-admiral, they went in the midst … and there went on each side, in the wings, their galleasses, armados of Portugal, and other good ships, in the whole to the number of sixteen in a wing, which did seem to be of their principal shipping.' In other words, they resumed their old defensive posture, with a centre protected by a rearguard, and flanked by two powerful wings. The supply hulks took up position in front of the Armada, between the warships and the English.

Shortly after 1000hrs Drake launched the first close-range attack in the *Revenge*, leading his squadron towards the Armada's left (western) wing. Soon Sir John Hawkins joined the battle with his squadron, echeloned on Drake's right. One of his ships was the *Mary Rose*, and an observer on board noted: 'As soon as we that pursued the fleet were come up within musket shot of them, the fight began very hotly.'

Behind Hawkins and probably further to the east came Sir Martin Frobisher's squadron. All three squadrons began a fierce close-range engagement, with the Spanish ships continually trying to board their

One of the most popular representations of the Armada battle. In the foreground is a Spanish galleass, one of four which include the *San Lorenzo* and the *Girona*. The English and Spanish fleets engaged, 1588. Oil painting, English school, late 16th century. (NMM – BHC0262)

English assailants and the smaller Tudor warships trying to avoid coming too close. Once again the battle was fought within musket shot, so that the English gunnery advantage could be used to its greatest effect. The battle soon degenerated into what appeared to observers to be a general mêlée. This was an illusion, since although the English attacks were causing massive damage to individual Armada ships, the integrity of the Spanish battle formation remained largely intact.

During the late morning the English were reinforced by stragglers returning from the action against the *San Lorenzo* off Calais. Seymour led these ships in an assault on the unengaged right (east) flank of the Armada formation, so that by noon the entire Armada formation was engaged in the battle. Over on the left flank Sir William Winter reported firing at 120 paces, and that the English fire caused the left wing of the Armada to crowd in towards the centre, repeating the tendency first shown in the battle off Plymouth. He also claimed that four of the Spanish warships collided with each other and were badly damaged.

Howard rejoined his fleet at around 1300hrs the Spanish formation was showing signs of disintegration. Howard engaged the Spanish rearguard. As a witness recorded, 'My Lord Admiral with the rest of the fleet came up and gave a very fresh onset.' The damage and casualties were concentrated in the most powerful of the Spanish warships, the galleons and *naos* which had formed the 'van' or rearguard during the fighting in the Channel. Witnesses claimed that by the end of the battle some of these ships were so low in powder and shot that the only reply to the English barrage was small-arms fire.

Evidence from Armada shipwrecks tells a different story. Spanish guns were slow to reload, and any attempt to do so would have disrupted the organisation of the ship. The Spanish posted one gunner to each large gun, assisted by six or more soldiers. Once the gun had been fired, the soldiers would return to their normal duty, which was to wait for a

LEFT **Depiction of the Battle off Gravelines. Engraving of the Flemish School, late 16th century. Several aspects of the battles off Calais and Gravelines are incorporated into the picture, including the attack by the English fireships in the middle distance. (Author's collection)**

THE *SAN MARTIN* AT GRAVELINES

Dawn on 8 August found the Armada drifting between Calais and the Banks of Flanders. In disarray following a night-time fireship attack, the fleet was completely vulnerable, and the English fleet closed with them to give battle. The Duke of Medina Sidonia in his fleet flagship *San Martin* lay between the two fleets, and formed a rallying point for four other galleons, including Recalde's *San Juan*. These five galleons met the brunt of the English attack and held them off for two long hours, buying time for the rest of the Armada to regroup into a defensive formation.

Fortunately for the Spaniards, half of the English fleet were trying to capture the damaged galleass *San Lorenzo* off Calais. The remaining ships were unable to capture the galleons or even break through to reach the main Spanish fleet. The *San Martin* eventually fought her way back to the protection of the rest of the Armada, badly battered. Her hull had been pierced over 200 times, and her decks were reportedly running with blood, but the galleon was unbowed, a testimony to the bravery of the Spanish crew. The plate depicts the *San Martin* towards the end of this action, with the surrounding English warships firing at her from within 'range of a pistol shot'.

A Spanish galleass (probably the *San Lorenzo*) being attacked by small English boats off Calais (8 August 1588). Detail from *The Battle off Gravelines*, one of a series of engravings of the House of Lords Armada Tapestries, which were destroyed by fire in 1834. Engraving by John Pine, c.1739. (NMM)

OPPOSITE **Close-up of the Battle off Gravelines, seen from the romantic viewpoint of a late 18th-century Anglo-Polish maritime artist. *Defeat of the Spanish Armada*, an oil painting by Philip James de Loutherbourg (1740-1812). Although the battle was fought at close range, there were no attempts made to board enemy vessels during the fighting. (NMM, London – GH26, on loan to Greenwich Hospital)**

boarding action. In order to reload they would have to lay aside their weapons and manhandle a gun on an awkward two-wheeled carriage. In the 15 minutes or so it would have taken for a skilled crew to reload a Spanish culverin, a similar-sized gun and crew using an English four-wheeled truck carriage could have fired two or three times. On the other hand, evidence from the Armada shipwrecks suggests that these ships had expended almost all of their close-range armament of light guns and swivel guns ('versos'). In other words, the smaller the gun, the more likely it was to have been fired. This supports the English assertion that the fighting off Gravelines was fought at very close range. As Sir William Winter stated: 'When I was furthest off in discharging any of the pieces, I was not out of the shot of their harquebus, and most times within speech of one another.' One of the galleons on the Armada's left (west) flank was the *San Felipe*, and when her commander, Don Francisco de Toledo, tried to board an English ship, the enemy were close enough for Spanish soldiers to fire on to her decks before the English vessel turned away.

Medina Sidonia scraped together what reserves he could find and formed a new rearguard, probably led by Don Alonso de Leiva in *La Rata Santa María Encoronada* and Juan Martinez de Recalde in the battered *San Juan de Portugal*. His aim was to protect the more battered ships of the Armada and shepherd the fleet away to the north-east. The three Portuguese galleons – the *San Mateo*, *San Felipe* and *San Luis* – were among the most badly battered ships in the Armada, apart from Medina Sidonia's *San Martín*. According to a Spaniard, the *San Juan de Sicilia* was damaged so heavily by English fire that she was forced to 'repair the damage from many shots which the ship had received alow and from the

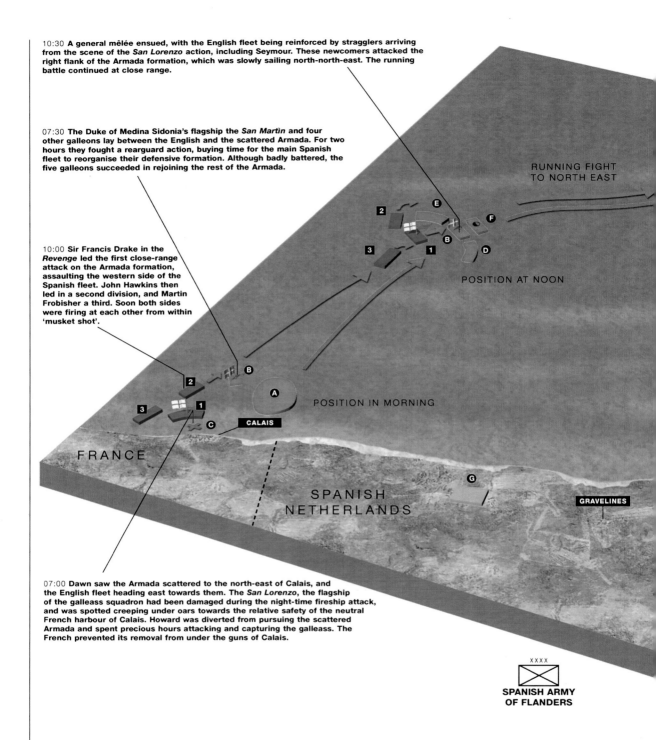

10:30 A general mêlée ensued, with the English fleet being reinforced by stragglers arriving from the scene of the *San Lorenzo* action, including Seymour. These newcomers attacked the right flank of the Armada formation, which was slowly sailing north-north-east. The running battle continued at close range.

07:30 The Duke of Medina Sidonia's flagship the *San Martìn* and four other galleons lay between the English and the scattered Armada. For two hours they fought a rearguard action, buying time for the main Spanish fleet to reorganise their defensive formation. Although badly battered, the five galleons succeeded in rejoining the rest of the Armada.

10:00 Sir Francis Drake in the *Revenge* led the first close-range attack on the Armada formation, assaulting the western side of the Spanish fleet. John Hawkins then led in a second division, and Martin Frobisher a third. Soon both sides were firing at each other from within 'musket shot'.

RUNNING FIGHT TO NORTH EAST

POSITION AT NOON

POSITION IN MORNING

CALAIS

FRANCE

SPANISH NETHERLANDS

GRAVELINES

07:00 Dawn saw the Armada scattered to the north-east of Calais, and the English fleet heading east towards them. The *San Lorenzo*, the flagship of the galleass squadron had been damaged during the night-time fireship attack, and was spotted creeping under oars towards the relative safety of the neutral French harbour of Calais. Howard was diverted from pursuing the scattered Armada and spent precious hours attacking and capturing the galleass. The French prevented its removal from under the guns of Calais.

xxxx
SPANISH ARMY OF FLANDERS

BATTLE OF GRAVELINES (THE DECISIVE CLOSE-RANGE ENGAGEMENT), 8 AUGUST, 1588

Viewed from the Flemish Coast (south), this decisive fight took the form of a running battle, heading from the Calais Roads north around the Banks of Flanders and into the North Sea. The relative positions of all elements of the two fleets have been shown at various crucial stages of the engagement.

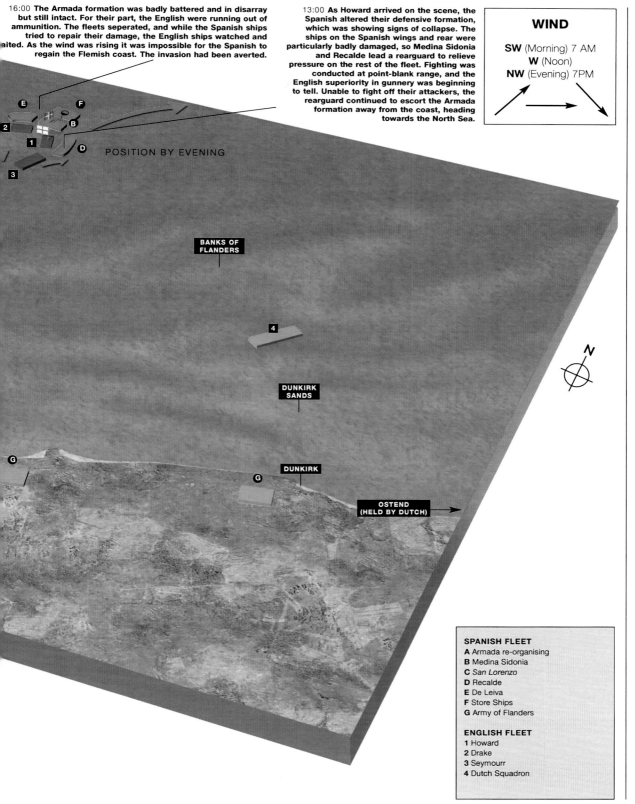

16:00 The Armada formation was badly battered and in disarray but still intact. For their part, the English were running out of ammunition. The fleets seperated, and while the Spanish ships tried to repair their damage, the English ships watched and waited. As the wind was rising it was impossible for the Spanish to regain the Flemish coast. The invasion had been averted.

13:00 As Howard arrived on the scene, the Spanish altered their defensive formation, which was showing signs of collapse. The ships on the Spanish wings and rear were particularly badly damaged, so Medina Sidonia and Recalde lead a rearguard to relieve pressure on the rest of the fleet. Fighting was conducted at point-blank range, and the English superiority in gunnery was beginning to tell. Unable to fight off their attackers, the rearguard continued to escort the Armada formation away from the coast, heading towards the North Sea.

WIND

SW (Morning) 7 AM
W (Noon)
NW (Evening) 7PM

POSITION BY EVENING

BANKS OF
FLANDERS

DUNKIRK
SANDS

DUNKIRK

OSTEND
(HELD BY DUTCH)

SPANISH FLEET

A Armada re-organising
B Medina Sidonia
C *San Lorenzo*
D Recalde
E De Leiva
F Store Ships
G Army of Flanders

ENGLISH FLEET

1 Howard
2 Drake
3 Seymourr
4 Dutch Squadron

71

ABOVE **Fragment of a pennant (1588) from the Portugal Squadron galleon *San Mateo* (750 tons). The Spanish galleon was heavily damaged during the Battle off Gravelines and was captured by the Dutch the following day. The painted linen banner hung in a church in Leiden for almost 300 years after the battle. (Stedelijk Museum, Leiden)**

RIGHT **The Battle off Gravelines, from *The Armada's progress from Plymouth to Gravelines*. Engraving by Claes Jansz. Visscher. Although fought as a close-range engagement, the Spanish fleet managed to maintain more of a defensive formation. The loose mêlée depicted in the print is therefore rather fanciful. (NMM 8.35)**

prow to the stern'. A Spaniard on board the *San Salvador* reported: 'The enemy inflicted such damage upon the galleons *San Mateo* and *San Felipe* that the latter had five guns on the starboard side and a big gun on the poop put out of action.'

By late afternoon the two warships were forced to fall out of the Armada formation, and drifted off towards the Banks of Flanders to the south and east. During the night they grounded close to the Flemish coast and were captured by the Dutch coastal fleet. One other Spanish ship was lost during the day. The nao *La María Juan* of the Biscay

Squadron was sunk by the concentrated fire of several English ships. She went down as negotiations to surrender were under way, and only one boatload of men escaped.

By 1600hrs the ferocity of the battle had begun to diminish, as the English ships became increasingly short of powder and shot. Accounts listing some of the armed merchant vessels which accompanied Seymour's squadron say the ships only carried 20 rounds for each gun, plus a few extra rounds of barshot (to cut down rigging) and 'diced shot' (a form of grapeshot). Sir William Winter estimated that his ship,

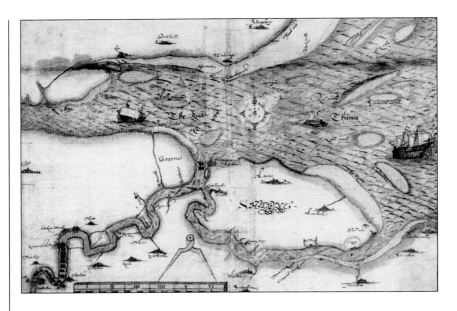

Chart of the Medway and the mouth of the Thames. Pen and wash, c.1580. This was the last chance for the Armada to find a secure anchorage and landing site. If the rendezvous with the Duke of Parma's army had been achieved, a landing near the Isle of Sheppey (foreground) would have been highly likely. (Hatfield House, CPM II/47)

Vanguard, fired over 500 rounds, roughly 12 shots per gun. As the battle had already lasted over eight hours, this was hardly surprising.

Although the Spanish Armada was badly battered during the day and its formation was in some disarray, it remained intact as a fleet. The English slowly fell behind the Spanish rearguard, and as firing died away both sides tried to repair the damage they had suffered. The lack of ammunition was a grave concern to Howard and the other English commanders, who thought their fleet would be unable to renew the fight unless more munitions were brought from England. For his part, Medina Sidonia was perfectly willing to renew the battle the next day, as it was the only way he would be able to link up with the Duke of Parma. He must also have been aware that the English were short of ammunition. Spanish casualties had been heavy – estimated at around 1,000 killed and 800 wounded – but Spanish morale was still high.

It was the wind that sealed the Armada's fate. In the early evening a strong north-westerly sprang up, threatening to push the Armada ships back towards the Banks of Flanders. As darkness fell, Medina Sidonia's advisers suggested heading north-north-east into the safety of the North Sea. Instead he preferred to wait for morning, so he ordered his ships to try to maintain their position. Through the rest of the night the Armada edged closer to the Banks of Flanders, and the Duke sent experienced pilots throughout the fleet in small pinnaces, advising the ships to stay as close to the wind as possible.

At dawn on Tuesday 9 August the two fleets were within a mile of each other, somewhere to the north of the sandbanks, some 25 miles north-north-east of Calais. Once again the *San Martín* was

BELOW **The Defeat of the Armada:** *Elizabeth I at Tilbury.* Oil on wooden panel, English School, early 17th century. Queen Elizabeth is depicted reviewing her troops at Tilbury following the defeat of the Armada, shown burning in the background. (St. Faith Church, Gaywood, near King's Lynn, Norfolk)

closest to the enemy, supported by five large warships and the remaining three galleasses. Medina Sidonia formed a rearguard that turned to face the English, but by that time the wind had died away almost completely, and Spanish morale was at last starting to break, causing him to accuse several of his captains of cowardice. One of these men was hanged a few days later.

For their part the English were willing to wait and see what happened, since the tide was still carrying the Armada towards the Banks of Flanders. Just when disaster seemed inevitable, the wind sprang up again, this time from the south-west. It allowed the Spaniards to claw themselves away from the sandbanks, but it also made it impossible to approach the English fleet. As his ships drifted north-east, the Duke called another council of war. He expressed his desire to return to Calais if the weather permitted, but he realised that if the breeze continued to freshen, he would be drawn further and further away into the North Sea. His more experienced naval commanders thought it almost impossible that they would be able to defy wind, tide and the English fleet and regain their anchorage off Calais. By the end of the meeting, it had been decided that there was little option but to continue on into the North Sea, then circumnavigate the British Isles in order to return to La Coruña.

Throughout the day the ships tried to prepare themselves for the long voyage home, and the bread, water and other victuals were redistributed throughout the Armada. For the most part the fleet was still intact, and although it faced a long voyage around Scotland and Ireland, the Armada was still a viable force, which could fight another day. The planned invasion of England would have to be postponed for another year. Unbeknown to both Medina Sidonia and Howard, a storm was forming in the Atlantic which would decimate by means of natural fury the fleet which English gunnery failed to destroy.

AFTERMATH

The decision by the Duke of Medina Sidonia to return to Spain by way of the North Sea and the Atlantic Ocean was based on a sound grasp of the strategic situation. Unable to return to Calais or sail up the Channel due to contrary winds, he had little option. On 12 August he determined a course for the entire fleet which took it around the Shetlands into the Atlantic, then, giving the Irish coast a wide berth, it would steer south towards La Coruña. The North Sea journey was an unpleasant one: temperatures dropped and fog banks and squalls disrupted the unity of the fleet. The English fleet was short of ammunition and supplies, but Lord Howard followed the Spanish as they sailed north, although he ordered Seymour's squadron back to the Downs to shield against any further invasion attempt by the Duke of Parma. The watershed for the English came on 12 August. The Armada had travelled the whole east coast of England without attempting to land, so when the Spanish passed the Firth of Forth in Scotland, Howard ordered his ships to turn back to the ports of north-east England. He simply lacked the supplies to stay at sea any longer.

Most of the Spanish fleet remained together, trying to make headway against a strong north-westerly wind, veering to the south-west for days on end. Medina Sidonia's flagship and the bulk of the fleet passed between Orkney and Shetland on 20 August and entered the Atlantic. By then the wind had changed to a north-easterly, ideal for running past the northern coast of Ireland before heading south for Spain. A day later the Duke sent a pinnace flying ahead with news of the Armada's progress. Other parts of the fleet were not so fortunate. As North Sea squalls turned into light gales, ships were driven as far east as the Norwegian coast and as far north as the Faroe Islands. On entering the Atlantic, most ships held a west-south-westerly course from Fair Isle, but the poor-sailing hulks and the most damaged ships were unable to hold such a southerly course and were forced further north.

By 24 August the wind had freshened and veered from the south. As a Spanish officer recalled: 'From the 24th to the 4th September we sailed without knowing whither, through constant storms, fogs and squalls.' The bad weather caused the fleet to scatter a little, and the damage caused by the English gunnery placed strains on the seams and hulls of the most badly battered ships. As their seams opened up ships started to founder, including *La Barca de Hamburg*, whose crew were transferred to *La Trinidad Valencera*. To avoid further ships opening their hulls, others could just sail where the wind took them. On 3 September Medina Sidonia wrote: 'I pray God in his mercy will grant us fine weather so that the Armada may soon enter port; for we are so short of provisions that if for our sins we are long delayed, all will be irretrievably lost. There are now a great number of sick and many die.'

By the second week in September Medina Sidonia was somewhere to the west of Ireland, with the rest of the fleet scattered for hundreds of

Navigator's astrolabe recovered from the wreck of the *Girona*. While devices such as these allowed the Armada navigators to determine latitude with some accuracy, longitude was a result of guesswork. Poor charts and bad weather led to navigational errors which accounted for many of the Armada shipwrecks on the Irish coast. (Ulster Museum, Belfast)

DRAVN AFTER THE QVICKE

miles north. The wind was changing direction almost daily, and with no chance to estimate their position, most of the Spanish had no accurate idea of their location. The worst storm struck on 12 September, a gale which roared up from the south and scattered the fleet even further. Although Medina Sidonia and the main body of the fleet passed the southernmost tip of Ireland by 14 September with about 60 ships, the rest of the fleet remained somewhere off the Irish coast.

One by one, the leaking or sinking ships gave up and ran inshore, trying to find shelter on the Irish coast. One of the first was the *La Trinidad Valencera*, which beached in Kinnagoe Bay in Donegal. The ship broke up two days later, but most of the crew had managed to reach the shore, where they found themselves at the mercy of the Irish. The survivors were duly captured by an English patrol, and all but the senior officers were massacred. A similar fate befell other shipwreck survivors from Ulster to County Kerry. The three Levant Squadron ships – the *Lavia*, *Juliana* and *Santa María de Visón* – anchored off Streedagh Strand in County Sligo. A few days later another westerly gale hit them, driving the ships ashore. Over 600 bodies were washed up on the beach, and those that survived were stripped and killed by the English and their Irish auxiliaries. Only a handful escaped into the hinterland, and most of these were captured and executed. This second gale, on 21-25 September, finished off many of the leaking Armada ships, including the *La Santa María de la Rosa*, which sank off County Kerry, and *El Gran Grin*, which was wrecked off Connaught.

Perhaps the worst tragedy was the loss of Don Alonso de Leiva. He survived the wrecking of his flagship *La Rata Santa María Encoronada* in Blacksod Bay (County Mayo) on 21 September and transferred his men to

A late 16th-century representation of Irish warriors, indicative of the men who looted many of the Armada's survivors as they struggled ashore on the Irish coast. Local chieftains then passed or sold the shipwrecked Spaniards on to the English. (Ashmolean Museum, Oxford).

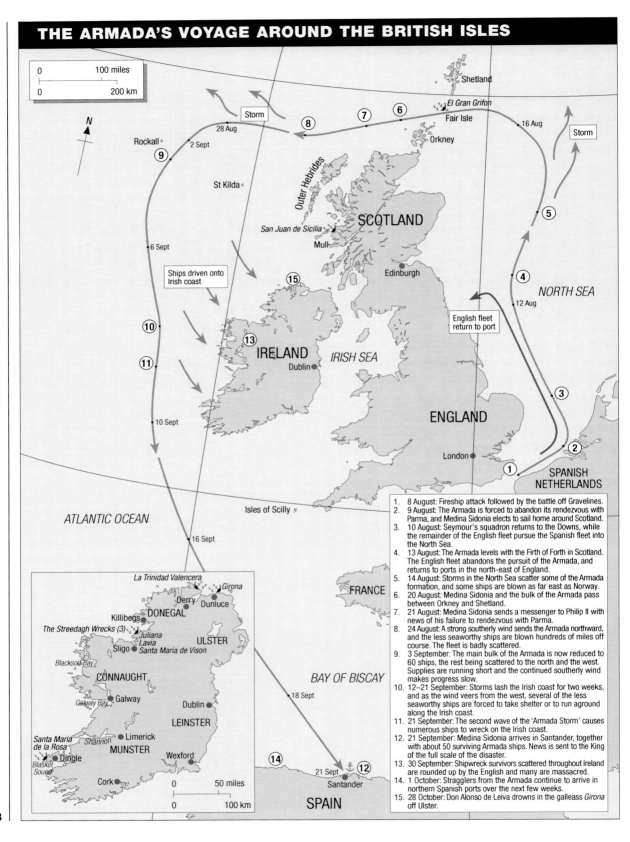

THE ARMADA'S VOYAGE AROUND THE BRITISH ISLES

0   100 miles
0   200 km

N

Shetland

El Gran Grifon
Fair Isle

Orkney

16 Aug

Storm

Storm

28 Aug

2 Sept

Rockall

6 Sept

St Kilda

Outer Hebrides

SCOTLAND

Edinburgh

San Juan de Sicilia
Mull

Ships driven onto
Irish coast

English fleet
return to port

12 Aug

NORTH SEA

IRELAND

IRISH SEA

Dublin

10 Sept

ENGLAND

London

16 Sept

SPANISH
NETHERLANDS

ATLANTIC OCEAN

Isles of Scilly

1. **8 August:** Fireship attack followed by the battle off Gravelines.
2. **9 August:** The Armada is forced to abandon its rendezvous with Parma, and Medina Sidonia elects to sail home around Scotland.
3. **10 August:** Seymour's squadron returns to the Downs, while the remainder of the English fleet pursue the Spanish fleet into the North Sea.
4. **13 August:** The Armada levels with the Firth of Forth in Scotland. The English fleet abandons the pursuit of the Armada, and returns to ports in the north-east of England.
5. **14 August:** Storms in the North Sea scatter some of the Armada formation, and some ships are blown as far east as Norway.
6. **20 August:** Medina Sidonia and the bulk of the Armada pass between Orkney and Shetland.
7. **21 August:** Medina Sidonia sends a messenger to Philip II with news of his failure to rendezvous with Parma.
8. **24 August:** A strong southerly wind sends the Armada northward, and the less seaworthy ships are blown hundreds of miles off course. The fleet is badly scattered.
9. **3 September:** The main bulk of the Armada is now reduced to 60 ships, the rest being scattered to the north and the west. Supplies are running short and the continued southerly makes progress slow.
10. **12–21 September:** Storms lash the Irish coast for two weeks, and as the wind veers from the west, several of the less seaworthy ships are forced to take shelter or to run aground along the Irish coast.
11. **21 September:** The second wave of the 'Armada Storm' causes numerous ships to wreck on the Irish coast.
12. **21 September:** Medina Sidonia arrives in Santander, together with about 50 surviving Armada ships. News is sent to the King of the full scale of the disaster.
13. **30 September:** Shipwreck survivors scattered throughout Ireland are rounded up by the English and many are massacred.
14. **1 October:** Stragglers from the Armada continue to arrive in northern Spanish ports over the next few weeks.
15. **28 October:** Don Alonso de Leiva drowns in the galleass *Girona* off Ulster.

FRANCE

BAY OF BISCAY

18 Sept

21 Sept

Santander

SPAIN

La Trinidad Valencera

Girona

Derry

Dunluce

DONEGAL

Killibegs

The Streedagh Wrecks (3)
Juliana
Lavia
Sligo
Santa Maria de Vison

ULSTER

Blacksod Bay

CONNAUGHT

Galway

Galway Bay

Dublin

LEINSTER

Santa Maria
de la Rosa
Shannon
Limerick

MUNSTER

Wexford

Blasket
Sound
Dingle

Cork

0   50 miles
0   100 km

LEFT **Following the Battle off Gravelines, it became clear that the Armada would be unable to rendezvous with the Duke of Parma's invasion force. Due to the prevailing westerly wind, Medina Sidonia was unable to return up the Channel, so he had little option but to order the Armada to return to Spain by sailing around the north of the British Isles. The English fleet pursued them as far as the Firth of Forth, when they returned to ports in north-eastern England to replenish their exhausted supplies. Storms in the North Sea scattered the Armada, although the bulk of the formation managed to regroup off Orkney, and Medina Sidonia led his fleet into the North Atlantic on 20 August. Further storms hit the fleet from the south, forcing some of the least seaworthy and badly damaged ships to run with the wind, and consequently dozens of ships were scattered to the north. Medina Sidonia led the remaining 60 ships on a southerly course, making slow progress against the prevailing winds. Supplies were running low throughout the fleet, and scurvy and malnutrition were rife. On 12 September as Medina Sidonia passed clear of the Irish coast a fresh storm blew from the west causing many of the stragglers to be driven towards that coast. Over the next two weeks ship losses mounted. While Medina Sidonia's flagship reached the safety of the Spanish port of Santander on 21 September, many of the Armada vessels were not so fortunate. While dozens more straggled into Spanish ports over the next few weeks, dozens more were dashed against the Irish coast and wrecked. At least 45 Spanish ships were lost during the campaign, together with approximately 11,000 men.**

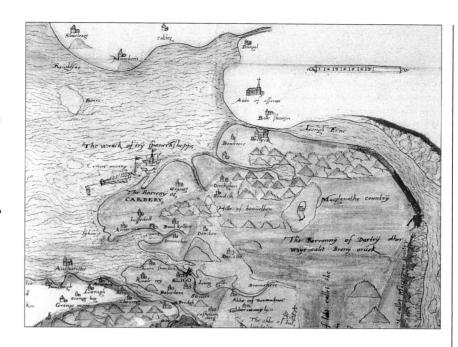

Detail from a map of County Sligo, Ireland, dated April 1589. Off the coast of Streedagh Strand the cartographer has shown 'the wrack of try Spanesh shepps'. These were *La Juliana* (860 tons), *La Lavia* (728 tons) and *Santa María de Visón* (666 tons), all from the Levant Squadron. The wrecks were discovered in 1985. (PRO, London – MPF 91)

the *Duquesna Santa Anna*. He put to sea, but another gale drove this second ship ashore in Donegal. Don Alonso and the other survivors marched overland to Killibegs on Donegal Bay, where he found the galleass *Girona*. The commander supervised repairs to the ship for three weeks, then elected to continue north around Ulster to Scotland and a neutral harbour. The galleass was crammed with 1,300 men: the survivors of two shipwrecks as well as the original crew. On 28 October the *Girona* damaged her rudder fighting through heavy seas off Dunluce in Ulster. In the face of a northern gale and heavy seas the galleass was helpless, and she struck Lacada Point, a rocky outcrop at the base of a 400-foot cliff. All but a handful of the crew perished, including Don Alonso.

The first Armada ships began to straggle into the northern Spanish ports from 21 September and news of the disaster was sent to King Philip II. Most of the crew were suffering from advanced scurvy and malnutrition, while the incapacitated Medina Sidonia retired to his estates. Juan Martinez de Recalde survived to reach Bilbao, only to die a few weeks later while in a monastery hospital. As news of the losses mounted, the full extent of the disaster made itself apparent. In all, 65 ships made it back to Spain, which meant that at least 45 were lost, including 27 of the most prominent and largest ships in the Armada. Philip II was devastated by the loss, and was particularly affected by the death of his favourite, Don Alonso de Leiva. In early November it was reported that he prayed for death and underwent a crisis in his usually unshakeable faith.

The English propagandists had a field day, combining the success of the campaign in the Channel and the storms of September as proof that

RIGHT **Weather map reconstructed from contemporary accounts, showing the gale which caused so many of the battered Armada ships to founder or become shipwrecked. By 21 September the storm centre had been moving slowly north for a week, keeping parallel to the Irish coast. (Author's collection)**

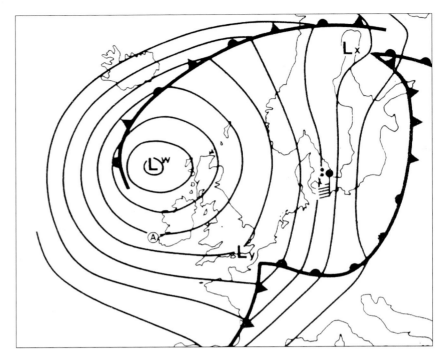

BELOW *The Somerset House Conference*. **Oil painting by Juan Pantoja de la Cruz, 1604. Peace between England and Spain was ratified in August 1604. In this painting the Spanish delegation sits on the left of the picture. Charles, Lord Howard of Effingham is the second figure from the window on the right. (NMM – BHC2787)**

THE SHIPWRECK OF THE *GIRONA*

Following the storm that scattered much of the Armada off the north coast of Ireland, the galleass *Girona* put into Killibegs in County Donegal. She spent much of October repairing the damage to her hull, and during this period her crew were joined by survivors from two other ships, the *Duquesa Santa Anna* (900 tons) and *La Rata Santa María Encoronada* (820 tons). On 26 October she sailed with over 1,300 men crowded on to her decks. The senior officer on board was Don Alonso Martínez de Leiva, the admiral commanding the Armada's vanguard division. As the ship was so unseaworthy he decided to sail east towards neutral Scotland rather than risk the Atlantic passage to Spain. She was off Dunluce in Antrim when her jury rudder broke and the heavy seas forced her against the rocks of Lacada Point, at the foot of a 400-foot cliff. Only five men survived the disaster. The plate depicts the final moments of the *Girona*, as the galleass breaks her back on the rocky promontory. Bodies littered the base of the cliffs the following morning. It was said that King Philip mourned the loss of Don Alonso more than the rest of the fleet. The wreck of the *Girona* was discovered in 1968 by Robert Sténuit, and all the artefacts recovered now reside in Ulster Museum, Belfast.

God favoured the Protestant cause. The English fleet had lost no ships and had suffered relatively minor damage. Elizabeth I was seen as the protector of the Reformation, and in the aftermath of the Armada campaign she sanctioned further attacks on Spain, and on the returning treasure fleets.

For his part Philip II galvanised the nation by ordering replacement ships, ordnance and men. As one of his councillors said: 'What matters is that we should show great courage, and finish what we have started.' However, his attempts to send a second Armada against England were defeated by bad weather in 1596 and 1597, and following Philip's death in 1598, any further invasion plans were abandoned. The death of Queen Elizabeth I in 1603 paved the way for peace negotiations, and the two sides duly met at Somerset House in London during 1604. A peace treaty was signed in August that year.

For the Spanish, the Armada marked the high-water mark of her political and military aspirations in Europe. The loss of prestige following the defeat of the Armada did Spain irreparable harm, and although the war with the Dutch would continue intermittently until 1648, Spain was increasingly seen as a secondary player in European politics. For the English, they emerged with a greatly enhanced reputation. Although the Armada had been defeated by fireships and storms rather than by the English navy, her status as a leading maritime power was assured, a position she would retain for the next three and a half centuries.

FURTHER READING

Only a selection of the many available works are listed below. For a more detailed bibliography, the exhibition catalogue *Armada 1588-1988* is highly recommended. In addition, numerous relevant articles have appeared in the *International Journal of Nautical Archaeology*, the *Mariners' Mirror* and other specialist publications.

Howard, F *Sailing Ships of War 1400-1860* (London, 1979)

Howarth, D *The Voyage of the Armada: The Spanish Story* (New York, 1981)

Laughton, JK (ed) *State papers relating to the defeat of the Spanish Armada*, 3 volumes (Navy Records Society, London, 1905)

Loades, D *The Tudor Navy: An Administrative, Political and Military History* (Aldershot, 1992)

McKee, A *From Merciless Invaders: The Defeat of the Spanish Armada* (London, 1963)

Martin, C *Full Fathom Five* (London, 1975)

Martin, C & Parker, G *The Spanish Armada* (London, 1988)

Mattingly, G *The Armada* (Boston, 1959)

Oppenheim, M *A History of the Administration of the Royal Navy from 1509 to 1660* (London, 1896; reprinted Aldershot, 1988)

Oppenheim, M *The Naval Tracts of Sir William Monson, Vol 1* (Navy Records Society, London, 1903)

Rodríguez-Salgado, MJ (ed) *Armada 1588-1988,* Exhibition Catalogue, National Maritime Museum, Greenwich (London, 1988)

Sténuit, R *Treasures of the Armada* (London, 1974)

Usherwood, S (ed) *The Great Enterprise: The History of the Spanish Armada as Revealed in Contemporary Documents* (London, 1982)

Walker, B *The Armada,* Time Life Seafarers Series (Amsterdam, 1982)

Waters, DW *The Elizabethan Navy and the Armada of Spain,* National Maritime, Monograph Series No.17, Greenwich (London, 1975)

BELOW *La Santa María de la Rosa* (945 tons), vice-flagship of the Guipúzcoan Squadron, was driven into Blasket Sound, County Kerry, and foundered in 120 feet of water. Her remains were discovered and excavated by Sid Wignall in 1968/9. (Dr Colin Martin)

THE ARCHAEOLOGICAL LEGACY

ABOVE **Stroms Hellier, the gully in Fair Isle where *El Gran Grifón* (650 tons) was wrecked. Most of the crew managed to scramble to safety up the masts and on to the cliff-top. Fifty of the survivors starved on the almost deserted island before help came. The wreck was discovered and excavated by Dr Colin Martin in 1970. (Dr Colin Martin)**

There is an old saying that 'No flowers bloom on a sailor's grave', but anyone who has dived on historic shipwrecks will contest this. There are no military cemeteries relating to the Spanish Armada campaign and no neatly preserved battlefields, while the English Channel, where the campaign was fought, is now one of the busiest shipping lanes in the world, particularly between Calais and Dover. What has survived over the centuries is evidence from shipwrecks, the remains of the Spanish Armada ships which held off the English fleet only to succumb to the elements off the coasts of Ireland and Scotland. Over 30 ships were known to have been lost during the storms which hit the Armada in September 1588.

At the time of publication, eight of these wrecks have been located and examined, and the information they have produced has greatly helped our understanding of the Spanish Armada, its ships and the men who sailed in them. In 1968 Sidney Wignall discovered the remains of the capitana of the Guipúzcoa Squadron, *La Santa María de la Rosa*. Over the next two years Wignall and a team of amateur archaeologists examined the remains of the vessel in the eye of a tidal rip 100 feet below the surface of Blasket Sound, County Kerry (south-west Ireland). At the same time Dr Robert Sténuit discovered and excavated the remains of the galleass *Girona* near Dunluce, County Antrim (Northern Ireland). There were 1,300 men on board when she sank, many of whom were survivors of two other shipwrecks. All but five were drowned, including Don Alonso de Leiva, one of the Armada's most celebrated commanders.

In 1970 Dr Colin Martin excavated the remains of the supply hulk *El Gran Grifón* at the base of a cliff in Fair Isle, a small island midway

RIGHT **The galleass *Girona* was wrecked on Lacada Point, a rocky promontory at the foot of a 400-foot-high cliff in County Antrim, Ireland. She was already carrying survivors from two other wrecks when she was cast ashore, and all but five of the 1,300 souls on board perished. The wreck was discovered and excavated in 1967/8. (Dr Colin Martin)**

ABOVE **A miscast and broken muzzle-end of a media culebrina from *El Gran Grifón* (now in the collection of the Shetland Museum, Lerwick). The miscast barrel is evidence of the poor quality and hasty production inherent in the Spanish gun-founding programme, which was stretched to the limit to accommodate the ordnance needs of the Armada. (Dr Colin Martin)**

ABOVE, LEFT **This Italian bronze sacre was recovered from the wreck of the *Juliana*, in Streedagh Strand, Ireland. A portion of the barrel appears to have been blown out, clear evidence that some of the guns carried on Armada ships were defective. (Dr Colin Martin)**

between Orkney and Shetland. Over the next few years he also worked in conjunction with the Derry Sub Aqua Club to excavate the remains of another hulk, *La Trinidad Valencera*, which broke up in Kinnagoe Bay, Country Donegal (north-west Ireland). In 1985 three more wrecks were discovered, the *Lavia*, *Juliana* and *Santa María de Visón*, all located off Streedagh Strand, County Sligo (eastern Ireland). Martin liaised with the divers who discovered the wrecks and with the Irish Government to uncover more vital information about the ships of the Spanish Armada.

The eighth wreck is the *San Juan de Sicilia*, which blew up at anchor in the remote Scottish harbour of Tobermory in Mull on 5 November 1588. Unfortunately little or nothing remains of the wreck after some four centuries of salvage and treasure-hunting.

No English warships have been located dating from this period. The *Mary Rose*, which sank in the Solent (off Portsmouth) in 1545 has yielded useful information on the ships and men of the Tudor navy. Another shipwreck discovered off Alderney in the Channel Islands was excavated during the 1980s and appears to have been a transport vessel, carrying men and munitions to the island around the time of the Armada campaign.

Taken together, the Spanish vessels cover many of the types which composed the Spanish Armada, from the 'fire brigade' ships which helped protect the rest of the fleet to the transport and supply vessels which carried soldiers and siege equipment, supplies and munitions. The *Girona* is unique as a galleass, a hybrid vessel that became obsolete shortly after the campaign. Unfortunately little remains of the hulls of these vessels, although the wreck site of *La Trinidad Valencera* yielded substantial organic and timber remains in good condition. Of all the objects recovered it is the ordnance carried on these Armada ships which offers the best insight into the campaign.

Artillery during the period was almost exclusively cast from bronze, although the English had begun experimenting with cast-iron production from the mid-16th century, and some vessels still used the older wrought-iron breech-loading guns, which were considered obsolete by 1588. Over 20 pieces of ordnance have been recovered from

TOP, LEFT **A gold cross of the Order of the Knights of the Hospice of St. John of Jerusalem, recovered from the wreck of the galleass *Girona*. It probably belonged to Fabricio Spinola, the vessel's captain. (Ulster Museum, Belfast)**

TOP, RIGHT **A gold salamander pendant recovered from the wreck of the *Girona*. It probably belonged to one of the ship's senior officers or a noblemen from one of the other** two ships whose crews she was carrying when she was wrecked. (Ulster Museum, Belfast)

BOTTOM **A Spanish siege-gun and reproduction carriage. The gun was carried on *La Trinidad Valencera* and was destined to form part of the Spanish landing force. The gun and the remains of the carriage were recovered from the shipwreck. (Dr Colin Martin)**

Armada wrecks and have been catalogued and classified by Martin and Parker (1988). Two significant features stand out: the range of nationalities and types of guns, and the variation in quality found among this sample, which is probably representative of the armament of the Armada as a whole. The German hulk *El Gran Grifón* was the capitana of the squadron of hulks, and carried 38 guns. Many of these were recovered during the archaeological excavation of the wreck, and they included a high proportion of wrought-iron guns. Significantly, one of the more modern bronze guns recovered (or at least a fragment of its barrel) showed it had been poorly cast and had a misplaced bore. Similar faults were found in other Armada guns, including a sacre (saker) from the *Juliana* that had a section of its bronze barrel blown out.

The equipping of the Armada was a vast undertaking which stretched the resources of Philip II to the utmost. Contemporary accounts mention hurried production of ordnance and may be indicative of a trend throughout the less powerful ships of the fleet. Gunners would be unwilling to risk firing these weapons more than necessary. Guns also came from a wide range of foundries: Flanders, Spain, Germany, Austria, Italy, France and Sicily. Of these, the German and Flemish guns had the reputation for excellence.

Even more revealing is an analysis of the shot recovered. By cross-referencing this with the shot recorded in manifests, we can gain a rough approximation of the number of shots fired. In a summary of all of the wrecks excavated before 1985, Martin (1988) demonstrated that while the large guns were not fired much during the campaign, the smaller swivel guns and breech-loading weapons were fired so much that ammunition stocks were low. This supports the notion that Spanish guns were mounted on unwieldy carriages, and therefore took an inordinately long time to reload. Although the navigational instruments, golden jewellery and coins recovered are of great interest, this information about the arming of the fleet is of far greater historical value, as it highlights the constraints faced by the Spanish gunners on board the Armada ships.

One further group of artefacts recovered from *La Trinidad Valencera* was particularly significant. The vessel carried part of a siege train, destined to support the Duke of Parma in his advance through Kent. The siege guns and their carriages, which were earmarked to be used against strongholds such as Dover Castle and the walls of London, were found virtually intact on the seabed off Donegal.

ORDER OF BATTLE

THE SPANISH ARMADA

Note: A capitana is a squadron flagship, and an almiranta is a second-in-command's ship. All vessels marked (*) were regarded as front-line vessels and were often deployed in a special 'van', a form of 'fire brigade' which could relieve pressure on threatened sections of the Armada formation.

SQUADRON OF PORTUGAL
Commander: The Duke of Medina Sidonia (who was also the Armada commander)

Ship Name	Ship Type	Tonnage	Guns	Crew	Fate
San Martín (Fleet Capitana)	Galleon (*)	1,000	48	469	Returned
San Juan de Portugal (Fleet Almiranta)	Galleon (*)	1,050	50	522	Returned
San Marcos	Galleon (*)	790	33	386	Lost
Florencia	Galleon (*)	961	52	383	Returned
San Felipe	Galleon (*)	800	40	439	Lost
San Luis	Galleon (*)	830	38	439	Returned
San Mateo	Galleon (*)	750	34	389	Lost
Santiago	Galleon	520	24	387	Returned
San Cristobal	Galleon	352	20	211	Returned
San Bernardo	Galleon	352	21	236	Returned
Augusta	Zabra	166	13	92	Returned
Julia	Zabra	166	14	135	Returned

SQUADRON OF BISCAY
Commander: Juan Martinez de Recalde (Also Armada Deputy Commander, with flag in San Juan). A nominal squadron commander in the Santiago commanded the squadron in Recalde's absence.

Ship Name	Ship Type	Tonnage	Guns	Crew	Fate
Santiago (Capitana)	Nao	666	25	312	Returned
El Gran Grin (Almiranta)	Nao (*)	1,160	28	336	Lost
La Concepción Mayor	Nao	468	25	219	Returned
La Concepción de Juan del Cano	Nao	418	16	225	Returned
La Magdalena	Nao	530	18	274	Returned
San Juan	Nao	350	21	190	Returned
La Maria Juan	Nao	665	24	399	Lost
La Manuela	Nao	520	12	163	Returned
Santa Maria de Montemayor	Nao	707	18	202	Returned
La Maria de Aguirre	Patache	70	6	43	Lost
La Isabela	Patache	71	10	53	Returned
La Maria de Miguel de Suso	Patache	96	6	45	Lost
San Esteban	Patache	78	6	35	Returned

Note: The original squadron capitana was the Santa Anna, but she was forced to seek shelter in a French port due to bad weather in the Bay of Biscay, and took no part in the campaign. The Santiago became the new capitana of the squadron.

Santa Anna de Juan Martinez	Nao (*)	768	30	412	

SQUADRON OF CASTILLE
Commander: Don Diego Flores de Valdés

Ship Name	Ship Type	Tonnage	Guns	Crew	Fate
San Cristóbal (Capitana)	Galleon (*)	700	36	303	Returned
San Juan Bautista (Almiranta)	Galleon (*)	750	24	296	Returned
San Pedro	Galleon	530	24	274	Returned
San Juan el Menor	Galleon	530	24	284	Lost

Ship Name	Ship Type	Tonnage	Guns	Crew	Fate
Santiago el Mayor	Galleon	530	24	293	Returned
San Felipe y Santiago	Galleon	530	24	234	Returned
La Asunción	Galleon	530	24	240	Returned
Nuestra Señora del Barrio	Galleon	530	24	277	Returned
San Medel y Celedón	Galleon	530	24	273	Returned
Santa Ana	Galleon	250	24	153	Returned
Nuestra Señora de Begoña	Galleon	750	24	300	Returned
La Trinidad	Nao	872	24	241	Lost
La Santa Catalina	Nao	882	24	320	Returned
San Juan Bautista ('Ferrandome')	Nao	652	24	240	Lost
Nuestra Señora del Socorro	Patache	75	12	35	Lost
San Antonio de Padua	Patache	75	12	46	Lost

SQUADRON OF ANDALUSIA
Commander: Don Pedro de Valdés

Ship Name	Ship Type	Tonnage	Guns	Crew	Fate
Nuestra Señora del Rosario (Capitana)	Nao(*)	1,150	46	559	Lost
San Fransisco (Almiranta)	Nao	915	21	323	Returned
San Juan Bautista	Galleon	810	31	333	Returned
San Juan de Gargarín	Nao	569	16	193	Returned
La Concepción	Nao (*)	862	20	260	Returned
Duquesna Santa Anna	Nao	900	23	273	Lost
Santa Catalina	Nao	730	23	289	Returned
La Trinidad	Nao	650	13	210	Returned
Santa María de Juncal	Nao	730	20	287	Returned
San Bartolomé	Nao	976	27	240	Returned
El Espírito Santo	Patache	70	6	33	Lost

SQUADRON OF GUIPÚZCOA
Commander: Miguel de Oquendo

Ship Name	Ship Type	Tonnage	Guns	Crew	Fate
Santa Anna (Capitana)	Nao (*)	1,200	125	400	Returned
Santa María de la Rosa (Almiranta)	Nao (*)	945	26	323	Lost
San Salvador	Nao (*)	958	25	371	Lost
San Esteban	Nao	936	26	274	Lost
Santa Marta	Nao	548	20	239	Returned
Santa Bárbara	Nao	525	12	182	Returned
San Buenaventura	Nao	379	21	212	Returned
La María San Juan	Nao	291	12	135	Returned
La Santa Cruz	Nao	680	18	165	Returned
La Urca Doncella	Nao	500	16	141	Returned
La Asunción	Patache	60	9	34	Lost
San Bernabé	Patache	69	9	34	Lost
Nuestra Señora de Guadalupe	Pinnace	-	1	12	Lost
La Madalena	Pinnace	-	1	14	Lost

SQUADRON OF THE LEVANT
Commander: Martín de Bertendona

Ship Name	Ship Type	Tonnage	Guns	Crew	Fate
La Regazona (Capitana)	Nao	1,200	30	371	Returned
La Lavia (Almiranta)	Nao (*)	728	25	302	Lost
La Rata Santa María Encoronada	Nao (*)	820	35	448	Lost
San Juan de Sicilia	Nao	800	26	332	Lost
La Trinidad Valencera	Nao (*)	1,100	42	413	Lost
La Anunciada	Nao	703	24	266	Lost
San Nicolas Prodaneli	Nao	834	26	294	Returned
La Juliana	Nao	860	32	412	Lost
Santa María de Vision	Nao	666	18	284	Returned
La Trinidad de Scala	Nao	900	22	408	Returned

SQUADRON OF HULKS (SUPPLY AND TRANSPORT SHIPS)

Commander: Juan Gómez de Medina

Ship Name	Ship Type	Tonnage	Guns	Crew	Fate
El Gran Grifón (Capitana)	Hulk	650	38	279	Lost
San Salvador (Almiranta)	Hulk	650	24	271	Returned
El Perro Marino	Hulk	200	7	96	Returned
El Falcon Blanco Mayor	Hulk	500	16	216	Returned
El Castillo Negro	Hulk	750	27	103	Lost
La Barca de Hamburg	Hulk	600	23	287	Lost
La Casa de Paz Grande	Hulk	600	26	-	Returned (*)
San Pedro el Mayor	Hulk	581	29	144	Lost
El Sansón	Hulk	500	18	125	Returned
San Pedro el Menor	Hulk	500	18	198	Lost
La Barca de Danzig	Hulk	450	26	178	Lost
El Falcón Blanco Mediano	Hulk	300	16	80	Lost
San Andres	Hulk	400	14	65	Returned
La Casa de Paz Chica	Hulk	350	15	175	Returned
El Ciervo Volante	Hulk	400	18	172	Lost
Paloma Blanca	Hulk	250	12	-	Returned (?)
La Buena Ventura	Hulk	160	4	64	Returned
Santa Bárbara	Hulk	370	10	130	Lost
Santiago	Hulk	600	19	65	Returned
David	Hulk	450	7	-	Returned (?)
El Gato	Hulk	400	9	71	Returned
San Gabriel	Hulk	280	4	47	Lost
Esayas	Hulk	260	4	47	Returned

Note: The crew levels of many of these vessels are unusually high because they were used to transport Spanish soldiers, reinforcements for the Duke of Parma's main amphibious landing force.

GALLEASS SQUADRON

Commander: Don Hugo de Moncada

Ship Name	Ship Type	Tonnage	Guns	Crew	Fate
San Lorenzo (Capitana)	Galleass (*)	-	50	368	Lost
Zúñiga	Galleass (*)	-	50	298	Returned
La Girona	Galleass (*)	-	50	349	Lost
Neopolitana	Galleass (*)	-	50	321	Returned

ATTACHED SMALL VESSEL SQUADRON

Commander: Augustín de Ojeda

Note: He succeeded Don Antonio Hurtado de Mendoza, who died during the voyage from Spain to the English coast. Only four of these vessels were over 100 tons:

Ship Name	Ship Type	Tonnage	Guns	Crew	Fate
Nuestra Senora del Pilar de Zaragoza	Nao	300	-	173	Lost
La Caridad Inglesa	Hulk	180	-	80	Returned (?)
San Andrés	Hulk	150	-	65	Returned (?)
El Santo Crusifijo	Patache	150	-	64	Lost

Of the remaining 34 vessels under 100 tons, ten were carvels, ten were pataches, seven were falúas and seven were zabras. Of these, at least nine were lost during the campaign and its aftermath.

An additional squadron of four galleys was forced to retire due to bad weather during the voyage from Spain to the English coast and took no part in the campaign.

THE ENGLISH FLEET

THE MAIN FLEET (PLYMOUTH)
Commander: Charles Howard, the Lord Admiral

Note: This includes the squadrons of Frobisher and Hawkins as well as the one directly controlled by Howard. No records survive which allow us to split the fleet down further into individual squadrons, probably because the commands were 'ad-hoc' and were never committed to paper. English records are less complete than those of the Spanish, and information on some vessels is not available. The total of guns includes all weapons over a 1-inch bore and comes from a list of 1585. Those marked (*) are derived from a list of 1602.

Royal Ships (14)

Ship	Commander	Tonnage	Guns	Crew
Ark Royal	The Lord Admiral	800	38*	430
Elizabeth	Bonadventure Earl of Cumberland	600	34	250
Golden Lion	Lord Thomas Howard	500	34	250
White Bear	Lord Sheffield	1,000	66	490
Elizabeth Jonas	Sir Robert Southwell	900	54	490
Victory	Sir John Hawkins	800	44	450
Triumph	Sir Martin Frobisher	1,100	46	500
Dreadnought	Sir George Beeston	400	26	190
Mary Rose	Edward Fenton	600	36	250
Swallow	Richard Hawkins	360	26	160
Foresight	Christopher Baker	300	26	150
Scout	Henry Ashley	100	18	80
Achates	Gregory Riggs	100	16	70
George Hoy	Richard Hodges	100	-	20

Armed Merchant Vessels (33)

Ship	Commander	Tonnage	Guns	Crew
Hercules of London	George Barne	300	-	120
Toby of London	Robert Barrett	250	-	100
Galleon	Dudley James Erisay	250	-	96
Centurion of London	Samuel Foxcraft	250	-	100
Minion of Bristol	John Sachfield	230	-	110
Mayflower of London	Edward Bancks	200	-	90
Ascension of London	John Bacon	200	-	100
Primrose of London	Robert Bringborne	200	-	90
Margaret & John of London	John Fisher	200	-	90
Tiger of London	William Caesar	200	-	90
Red Lion of London	Jervis Wilde	200	-	90
Minion of London	John Dale	200	-	90
Edward of Maldon	William Pierce	186	-	30
Gift of God of London	Thomas Luntlowe	180	-	80
Bark Potts	Anthony Potts	180	-	80
Bark Burr of London	John Serocold	160	-	70
Brave of London	William Furthow	160	-	70
Royal Defence of London	John Chester	160	-	80
Nightingale	John Doate	160	-	16
John Trelawney	Thomas Meek	150	-	30
Cure's Ship	-	150	-	-
Golden Lion of London	Robert Wilcox	140	-	70
Thomas Bonaventure of London	William Aldridge	140	-	70
Samuel of London	John Vassall	140	-	50
White Lion	Charles Howard	140	-	50
Crescent of Dartmouth	-	140	-	75
Bartholomew of Topsham	Nicholas Wright	130	-	70
Unicorn of Bristol	James Langton	130	-	66
Angel of Southampton		120	-	
Robin of Sandwich		110	-	
Galleon of Weymouth	Richard Miller	100	-	
John of Barnstable	-	100	-	65
Charity of Plymouth	-	100	-	

Howard also commanded the small royal ships *Charles* (70 tons, 8 guns) and *Moon* (60 tons, 13 guns), plus 87 smaller vessels of between 30 and 99 tons. Almost half were less than 50 tons, making them almost useless in battle. They were probably used to carry messages or stores, although little information is available on these small craft, the equivalent of the 45 pataches, zabras, falúas and carvels accompanying the Spanish fleet.

DRAKE'S SQUADRON (PLYMOUTH)

Commander: Sir Francis Drake

Royal Ships (5)

Ship	Commander	Tonnage	Guns	Crew
Revenge	Sir Francis Drake	500	36	250
Nonpareil	Thomas Fenner	500	34	250
Hope	Robert Crosse	600	33	280
Swiftsure	Edward Fenner	400	28	180
Aid	William Fenner	250	23	120

Armed Merchant Vessels (21)

Ship	Commander	Tonnage	Guns	Crew
Galleon Leicester	George Fenner	400	-	160
Merchant Royal	Robert Flicke	400	-	140
Roebuck	Jacob Whiddon	300	-	120
Edward Bonaventure	James Lancaster	300	-	120
Gold Noble	Adam Seager	250	-	110
Galleon Dudley	James Erisey	250	-	96
Hopewell	John Merchant	200	-	100
Griffin	William Hawkyns	200	-	100
Minion of London	William Winter	200	-	80
Thomas Drake	Henry Spindelow	200	-	80
Bark Talbot	Henry Whyte	200	-	80
Virgin God save Her	John Greynvile	200	-	70
Spark	William Spark	200	-	80
Hope Hawkins of Plymouth	John Rivers	180	-	70
Bark Mannington	Ambrose Mannington	160	-	80
Bark St. Leger	John St. Leger	160	-	80
Bark Bond	William Poole	150	-	70
Bark Bonner	Charles Caesar	150	-	70
Bark Hawkyns	William Snell	140	-	70
Elizabeth Founes	Roger Grant	100	-	60
Bear Yonge of London	John Yonge	140	-	70

Drake also commanded the small royal ship *Advice* (50 tons, 9 guns) plus 13 smaller vessels, of between 30 and 80 tons.

THE NARROW SEAS SQUADRON (OFF THE DOWNS)

Commander: Lord Henry Seymour

Royal Ships (7)

Ship	Commander	Tonnage	Guns	Crew
Rainbow	Lord Henry Seymour	500	24*	250
Vanguard	Sir William Winter	500	42*	250
Antelope	Sir Henry Palmer	400	24	170
Bull	Jeremy Turner	200	17	100
Tiger	John Bostocke	200	20	100
Tramontana	Luke Ward	150	21*	80
Scout	Henry Ashley	100	18	80

Armed Merchant Vessels (7)

Ship	Commander	Tonnage	Guns	Crew
William of Ipswich	Barnaby Lowe	140	-	50
Katharine of Ipswich	Thomas Grymble	125	-	50
Primrose of Harwich	John Cardinal	120	-	40
Elizabeth of Dover	John Litgen	120	-	70
Grace of Yarmouth	William Musgrave	150	-	70
Mayflower of Lynn	Alexander Musgrave	150	-	70
William of Colchester	Thomas Lambert	140	-	50

Seymour also commanded four small royal vessels: *Achates* (90 tons), *Merlin* (50 tons), *Sun* (39 tons) and *Cygnet* (29 tons). The *Spy*, *Fancy*, *George Hoy* and the *Bonavolia Galley* were detached on other duties. He also retained the use of 8 armed merchant vessels displacing 70 tons or less.

ENGLISH REINFORCEMENTS

Armed merchant vessels who voluntarily joined the English fleet during the campaign (6)

Ship	Commander	Tonnage	Guns	Crew
Sampson	John Wingfield	300	-	108
Frances of Fowey	John Rashley	140	-	60
Golden Ryall of Weymouth	-	120	-	50
Samaritan of Dartmouth	-	250	-	100
William of Plymouth	-	120	-	60
Grace of Topsham	Walter Edney	100	-	50

In addition, 15 smaller vessels under 90 tons also volunteered during the campaign.

Note: Most of these ships joined the fleet on 31 July and 1 August, during the fighting off the Devon coast.

Armed merchant vessels sent from London to reinforce Lord Seymour, 4 August 1588 (17)

Note: The first seven ships were commanded by Nicholas Gorges, Esquire, of London. The last ten ships were supplied by the Merchant Adventurers Guild of London, and were commanded by Henry Bellingham ('George Noble').

Ship	Commander	Tonnage	Guns	Crew
Susan Parnell of London	Nicholas Gorges	220	-	80
Violet of London	Martin Hawkes	220	-	60
Solomon of London	Edward Musgrave	170	-	80
Anne Francis of London	Charles Lister	180	-	70
George Bonaventure of London	Eleazer Hickman	200	-	80
Jane Bonaventure of London	Thomas Hallwood	100	-	80
Vineyard of London	Benjamin Cooke	160	-	60
George Noble of London	Richard Harper	120	14	60
Anthony of London	Richard Dove	100	12	50
Toby of London	Robert Cuttle	100	13	60
Salamander of Leigh	William Goodlad	110	12	55
Rose Lion of Leigh	Robert Duke	100	10	50
Antelope of London	Abraham Bonner	120	13	60
Jewel of Leigh	Henry Rawlyn	110	13	55
Pansy of London	William Butler	100	10	50
Prudence of Leigh	Richard Chester	120	12	60
Dolphin of Leigh	William Hare	110	11	55

Supply Vessels

Ship	Commander	Tonnage	Guns	Crew
Mary Rose	Francis Burnell	100	-	70
Elizabeth Bonaventure	Richard Start	100	-	60
Pelican	John Clarke	100	-	50
Hope	John Skinner	-	-	40
Unity	John Moore	-	-	40
Pearl	Lawrence Moore	100	-	50
Elizabeth of Leigh	William Bower	100	-	60
John of London	Richard Rose	100	-	70
Bearsabe	Edward Bryan	100	-	60
Marigold	Robert Bowers	100	-	50
White Hind	Richard Browne	-	-	40
Gift of God	Robert Harrison	100	-	40
Jonas	Edward Bell	100	-	50
Solomon	George Street	100	-	60
Richard Duffield	William Adams	100	-	70

These were despatched from the Thames Estuary to rendezvous with Howard's main fleet on 1 August. They reached Howard off the Isle of Wight on 3 August.

INDEX